MELONS & OTHER CUCURBITS

'*Cantalun*' melon

THE ENGLISH KITCHEN

MELONS
& OTHER CUCURBITS

GROWING & COOKING

RICHARD BROWN

PROSPECT BOOKS

2022

CONTENTS

Dedicated to my Mum, who inspired me to garden,
and my late Dad, who would have loved
every minute of this.

Young watermelon plants

Introduction

Without really realising it, I was engaged with gardening when I spent many childhood days outside in the large garden that my parents developed themselves, and which is still lovingly tended by my mum. I was in my twenties when, unfulfilled by an office-based job, I realised how attached to being outside I was, and that I needed to return to the creative and mental stimulation horticulture had given me.

I am also interested in many historical aspects of gardening, particularly Victorian walled gardens and the ability of their gardeners to produce fruits and vegetables from other climates in and out of season. I enjoy collecting, growing and saving seed of heritage varieties, particularly lettuce and peas, some of the old varieties of which can easily grow over two metres high.

I listened to gardening broadcaster Harry Dodson in the series *The Victorian Kitchen Garden* talk about the old varieties of vegetables they used to grow, some of which were nearly lost, then avidly researched them, found seed and grown them myself. One of the main features of the series was Harry's ability to cultivate melons under glass, where he grew '*Blenheim Orange*' and a variety new to me '*Hero of Lockinge*', both of which were bred by gardeners in England. I was soon captivated by this melon and tried to find seed of it. It quickly became obvious that the seed was no longer commercially available to buy, and it seemed as if it could not be sourced anywhere, not even the Heritage Seed Library were offering it. There were some suppliers in the US claiming to have stocks, but they did not ship to the UK. After weeks of searching, in a final throw of the dice, I searched social media for '*Hero of Lockinge*' and came across a Facebook group called 'Heirloom Cucurbits' where members shared information, grew, kept alive and shared seed of heritage varieties of melon, watermelon and squash. I posted a message saying I was looking for seed and I was promptly offered and sent some from a grower in southern Spain.

Awash with excitement at being able to grow and potentially save my own seed of this variety, which has teetered on the brink of being lost altogether, I set about growing it in isolation in my own greenhouse. Having grown melons before, I was aware of their requirements but at the back of my mind I was conscious this was an old variety bred and cultivated exclusively in heated Victorian glasshouses and that it had fallen out of favour for a reason, other than a criticism of flavour which has always been described as excellent. I soon found out why: in a summer that started out hot and dry, the plants suffered badly during a week in late June of overcast cool weather with recurrent overnight temperatures well below 10°C (one night even touched 5°C). The plants ceased flowering and wilted when the hot weather returned. They were knocked back so significantly that they ran out of time for enough fruit to set or ripen by late September. I needed to understand why. What had gone wrong? How could the technique be changed to ensure success? I set about reading various books, articles and websites, and after seeing 'If you can grow cucumbers and tomatoes you can grow melons' on more than one occasion, it became clear there was a lack of detailed advice specifically on growing melons and watermelons, especially in the UK and in other short season cold climates. I read through all the cultivation suggestions and went back to the successful methods I had used when I previously grew both types of melons in West Yorkshire. I trialled a range of different techniques and melon varieties to determine their requirements and how successful they were. I felt I wanted to share this information so that other gardeners who had been frustrated by their lack of success with melons in the past could revisit it, and those tempted to try them could avoid the failures others have had.

The other members of the cucurbit family are also a delight to grow and eat, so any book should also include these too. From this idea *Melons and Other Cucurbits* was born. I hope it will provide you with inspiration to grow these beautiful fruits, and give answers to previous problems that will encourage you to try again where things haven't gone quite to plan.

A ripe '*Hero of Lockinge*' melon

THE STORY OF THE MELON

ORIGINS

The melon, *Cucumis melo*, has troubled many scientists and historians trying to determine its history and exact origin. The seeds of melons and cucumbers look very alike, and there is such great diversity in fruit size and shape, from round and highly ribbed to long and smooth like a cucumber, that it makes them difficult to identify accurately from historical depictions.

There is still debate as to whether melons originated in Africa or the hot dry areas of the Middle East or India, with some research showing that the closest wild progenitor occurs in India. The flexuous group of *C. melo*, commonly known as snake melons, are long and thin, and look and taste like cucumbers. They were grown in Egypt at least 3,000 years ago and were the most common melon mentioned in historical literature. Arriving in Italy in the fifteenth century, via Armenia or Turkey, were the sweet tasting *Cantalupensis* group, which were named after Cantalupo, where they were grown at a papal country house. By 1518, melons of both the *Cantalupensis* and *reticulatus* groups (along with cucumbers and squash) were extensively included in Giovanni Martini da Udine's lavish frescos at Villa Farnesina in Rome, which show the range of melons and other cucurbits being cultivated in Italy at this time. The frescos have been fantastically well preserved and deserve a visit if you are in Rome. These were some of the earliest fruits introduced to the New World where they found a welcoming climate, with European settlers recorded as growing them in the 1600s. They spread, as did a lot of the more exotic edibles, through France and up to the UK, and by the Victorian period melons were being cultivated in the heated glasshouses of large estates. This generated an increasing demand for variety and quality, as demonstrated by Carter's seed catalogue of 1845 which had twenty-nine varieties of melon seed listed for sale, four of which are still available today: '*Emerald Gem*', '*Green Nutmeg*', '*Black Rock*' ('*Noir des Carmes*') and '*Queen's Pocket*' (or '*Queen Anne's Pocket*').

FRENCH HEIRLOOM MELON CULTIVATION: THE HOUSE OF VILMORIN-ANDRIEUX

Once melons arrived in Europe, they found a new home in the ideal climate and soil of Italy and France. This led to many new varieties being bred, particularly in France where the love and desire to grow them across the country led to melons that could cope with the cooler climate and shorter summers of the north, such as '*Noir des Carmes*', '*Petit Gris des Rennes*' and '*Prescott Hatif*' ('*Early Frame Prescott*'). These varieties were also suitable for, and eventually grown in, the UK.

The House of Vilmorin-Andrieux was founded in 1743 as a seed and plant boutique by the chief seed supplier and botanist to King Louis XV, Pierre Andrieux and his wife Claude Geoffroy. In 1774 their daughter married Phillipe-Victoire Levêque de Vilmorin and they revived the company's shops, renaming the company Vilmorin-Andrieux et Cie. By 1766 the seed house was importing trees and exotic plants, including melons, from around the world into Europe.

The firm also produced excellent seed catalogues with wonderful illustrations that have allowed heritage cucurbit enthusiasts to compare lost and misnamed varieties with ones from a hundred years or more ago. Without Vilmorin-Andrieux's drive to offer new seed and plants from around the world, not to mention their detailed and well-preserved documents that refer to them, it is likely that some of the heritage melons best suited to our climate would not have continued to survive.

The Premier Fruit of Victorian Britain and New Varieties

For some, wealth brings the ability to buy lavish and expensive items and to show off your success. For rich Victorians on their large estates it was no different, only for most of them it wasn't a sports car, a helicopter or yacht, it was plants. To own, be able to grow, or be the first to get a certain plant to flower, showed off your wealth and your skill (well, that of the head gardener), with the result that estates began to compete with each other. This fuelled plant hunting expeditions across the world that brought back exotic plants from Australia, China, Japan, India, Chile and many other countries, and encouraged attempts to cultivate them in the UK. Such was the desire to grow and protect these valuable specimens that huge glasshouses were built and heated at significant cost. This did not stop at ornamental plants, as serving your dinner guests peaches, grapes, pineapples and melons that had been grown on your own estate was the ultimate showcase of your status. Such was the kudos of these exotic table centrepieces that some houses, such as Cannon Hall in Barnsley, Yorkshire, rented out pineapples to be used for special dinner parties by owners who could not cultivate their own. It was, however, necessary to return them uneaten.

Melons were rightly high on the list of premier fruits of Victorian estates, which not only grew them, they also bred them on site and named them after the owners or estates of their creation. Sadly, many of these varieties are now lost forever (such as 'Sutton's Scarlet' pictured on the cover of this book), but two have survived: 'Blenheim Orange' and 'Hero of Lockinge'. These two melons were born at rival Oxfordshire estates less than twenty miles apart and competed against each other at numerous Royal Horticultural Society (RHS) fruit shows. 'Blenheim Orange' was bred by William Crump, head gardener to the Duke of Marlborough at Blenheim Palace, the birthplace of Winston Churchill. He introduced it to the public at the RHS show of 1880, where it duly won first prize, not only for having excellent flavour but also for being very productive and early to ripen. Carter's seed merchants were so enthused they bought the whole stock of seed from Crump and offered it exclusively a year later, describing it as 'the finest scarlet-fleshed melon in cultivation'. Not to be outdone, Mr Atkins, head gardener to Robert Loyd-Lindsay, the first Baron of Wantage, a founding member and first chairman of the British Red Cross, bred 'Hero of Lockinge' at Kitford Gardens, the walled kitchen garden of Lockinge House. Melon rivalry was not just confined to estates but also to seed houses, and Sutton's Seeds quickly bought the rights to the seed, introducing it as 'Sutton's Hero of Lockinge' at the 1881 RHS fruit show, where it beat William Crump's melon to first prize.

As the First and Second World Wars took their toll on finances and the young workforce, Victorian gardens slipped into decline, and so did the seed offerings of exotic and harder-to-grow fruits, as people focussed their attention on more reliable and staple crops during the 'Dig for Victory' campaign. In their 1940 seed catalogue Sutton's no longer had any melons or cucumbers listed for sale, and by 1950 they were notifying gardeners that due to 'enforced stoppage of propagation during the late war, and labour shortage, stocks in some cases are low'. *'Blenheim Orange'* remained popular and is available commercially to this day, but *'Hero of Lockinge'* was in real danger of becoming extinct, and without the seed saving of amateur gardeners and the excellent work carried out by the Heritage Seed Library, it would have been. In the UK, possibly due to it being a challenge to grow (it was born in coal-fired heated greenhouses after all), *'Hero of Lockinge'* is no longer available to buy. For those in North America, where it is still on offer, buy the seed, grow it, save it and love it.

Sliced watermelon

THE STORY OF THE WATERMELON

ORIGIN

In comparison to other continents Africa does not have a lot of edible plants, but coffee and watermelon (*Citrullus lanatus*) are arguably the most significant contributions. The exact history is still being deciphered but work carried out by Susanne Renner analysing the DNA of seeds, and Harry Paris' reviews of historical literature have pieced together its history and pinpointed that the closest relative to the fruit we know today is the Kordofan melon found in Sudan.

Originally, watermelons were thought to have descended from the Citron melon, *Citrullus lanatus* var. *citroides*, which is native to the Kalahari Desert. These are bitter to eat, but were prized for the water they contained. They could be harvested, carried long distances and then crushed to release the water for drinking. However, DNA analysis has proved that the Citron melon is not the ancestor to the modern-day watermelon.

Domestication of the watermelon goes back at least 5,000 years to Uan Muhuggiag, a pre-historic archaeological site in South West Libya, where seeds of the wild watermelon were found. 4,000-year-old paintings have been found in Egyptian tombs depicting an elongated striped watermelon served on a plate with other fruits, including grapes. This demonstrates that the Egyptians had selectively bred and cultivated fruit that was no longer bitter and had a hard flesh that required processing, but which was sweet and could be served fresh.

Through Harry Paris' work the trail of the watermelon can be seen in writings from 400 BC to 500 AD as it travelled into the Middle East and the Mediterranean countries. The Bible references watermelon as one of the fruits the Israelites longed for after leaving Egypt. Watermelons were also recorded in ancient manuscripts of Jewish law as items to be tithed. The Greek physicians Dioscorides and Hippocrates called it '*pepon*', and referred to its medicinal properties as a diuretic, and its use as a treatment for heat stroke in children by placing cool wet rinds on their heads. In the first century AD, Pliny the Elder, a Roman naturalist, noted in his *Historia naturalis* that the watermelon ('*pepo*' in Latin) was a good cooling food, '*refrigerant maxime*'.

The watermelon had moved to India by the seventh century and was growing in China by the tenth century. Its journey was no doubt facilitated, as with many fruits and crops, by the Silk Road, the famous network of trade routes that connected the West, through the Middle East, to China. The Moors took the watermelon with them when they invaded the Iberian Peninsula, where the soil and climate suited it perfectly.

The first illustrations of red-fleshed watermelon appear in the *Tacuinum Sanitatis* from the fourteenth century. This medical guide on the maintenance of health was written by Ibn Butlan in Baghdad. The Italians were very interested in this book and translated it into Latin, and then it was subsequently issued with many colour illustrations, including some of melons and oblong, green-striped watermelons with red flesh being harvested. By the seventeenth century it was being grown across Southern Europe, and Giuseppe Recco's *Still Life with Fruit and Flowers* (c. 1670) shows large red-fleshed watermelons alongside other sweet fruits which would be eaten fresh.

American Watermelons and the Slave Trade

The country most people probably associate with the watermelon is America, but the fruit is a relative newcomer to the country where it takes its home. It was transported across the Atlantic to the New World by European colonists and the slave trade. As slaves were taken from Western Africa to the cotton and tobacco plantations in the south-east of America, seeds and fruit were taken aboard ship with them. They found the perfect hot climate in the sandy, free-draining soil of the popular plantation states of Georgia, Florida and South Carolina, where they were grown in abundance. Georgia and Florida remain two of the largest commercial producing watermelon states in the US. The first cookbook published in America in 1796, *American Cookery* by Amelia Simmons, contained a recipe for pickled watermelon rind. Thomas Jefferson, a Founding Father and the third president of the United States, was a keen observer of the natural environment, and he trialled many fruits and vegetables at his home at Monticello, Virginia, to ascertain whether they would be useful food crops to support an increasing American population. He was a detailed note taker, and documented growing watermelons between 1770 and 1826.

The Watermelon War

In early 1800s America there was no direct land route linking the Atlantic and Pacific coasts, as the interior had not been developed or any railway laid. The only way to get from the east coast to the developing gold rush state of California was by boat, however sailing the length of South America and back up again was not only dangerous but very time consuming. The shortest land mass to cross was in Panama, which at the time was then part of the Republic of New Grenada. The United States entered into agreement with New Grenada that they could have transit rights to cross Panama in return for American assistance in protecting the Republic from potential European takeover. Crossing the interior of Panama quickly became troublesome as it required a boat ride up the Chagres River in native canoes, and the rest of the way on the back of mules through a jungle which often experienced high rainfall. Added to this was the risk of disease and local bandits, who frequently held up and robbed the American travellers. The solution was to build a 47-mile railway across Panama from Colón to Balboa, near Panama City. It was completed in 1855 and due to the difficult terrain and weather it was one of the most expensive American construction projects at the time in both cost and lives. It is said that between 5,000-10,000 workers died in the five years it took to install. The local bandits caused problems throughout the construction by holding up and stealing from the railway workers. Fed up with these constant issues and delays, the railway company hired a former Texas Ranger called Randolph Runnels, who, with the approval of both the New Grenada and American governments, formed a law enforcement group that patrolled the railway, hunting down local bandits. Reports describe that on multiple occasions Runnels had groups of bandits hung in the street as a warning to other would-be criminals, and this gave him a feared reputation and the nickname 'El Verdugo' ('The Executioner').

On 15th April 1856, a group of around a thousand mainly American passengers arrived on the Atlantic Coast of Panama to take a train across the country and onwards to San Francisco. One story goes that while waiting for the train to depart many passengers bought copious amounts of alcohol for the ride, either way, at the end of the five-hour cross country trip a lot of passengers disembarked the train in a worse state than when they got on. As Panama City was not a deep-water port, the onward boats were anchored in the bay, and the inebriated travellers had to wait four hours for a sufficiently high tide to transfer them by ferry. While waiting, one of the passengers, Jack Oliver, helped himself to a slice of watermelon from a street vendor and refused to pay for it. The vendor drew a knife on Oliver who in turn produced a revolver. A member of the crowd attempted to wrestle the revolver from Oliver and it went off, striking someone in the crowd. The locals, who were suffering from high unemployment and poverty – which they blamed on the Americans and the railway company for causing the loss of hotels, vendors and services along the previous river and road route – needed little encouragement for unrest and a riot ensued. American-owned businesses and hotels were attacked, as well as anyone suspected of being American. The travellers fled back to the train station for safety and were followed by locals and police. Some reports claimed that a shot was fired from the station, killing a police officer and causing a second eruption of violence. A telegraph was sent to other railway stations for help, and a train arrived with armed railway agents and a certain Randolph Runnels. The most romantic version of the story is that the mere presence of El Verdugo and his fearsome reputation was enough to quell the rioting locals; how true this is remains unclear but the riot did cease. When the dust had settled the US consul reported that fifteen Americans and two Panamanians were killed, with at least sixty wounded on both sides.

In the aftermath, investigations carried out by both governments laid the blame on each other. New Grenada admitted to failing to control the peace, and hundreds of thousands of dollars were awarded to American citizens in damages. The US sent 160 troops to take control of the railway station, which was the first of several future military interventions in Panama, and it subsequently established military bases on the islands off the Panama coast. The area remained strategically important to the US, which maintained a military presence in Panama from the time of the incident until 1999. And all of this was instigated by the refusal to pay no more than ten cents for a slice of watermelon.

THE BRADFORD WATERMELON: WORTH DYING FOR?

Sadly, the Bradford Watermelon is not related to the Yorkshire city famous for its textile mills but named after Nathaniel Bradford, a nineteenth-century watermelon farmer in Sumter, South Carolina, in America. Prior to the 1840s Nathaniel was growing watermelons including the '*Lawson*' which, the story goes, was named after a Georgia military officer who was captured during the American Revolutionary war and shipped to the West Indies to be imprisoned. While on board the ship a Scottish captain gave him a slice of watermelon, from which Lawson saved the seeds. On his return to Georgia he planted the seeds, which grew into sweet red-fleshed watermelons that became very popular. Nathaniel Bradford was one of only two other people that Lawson gave seeds to, the other grower went on to use the seeds to breed the famous '*Georgia Rattlesnake*' watermelon. Nathaniel crossed '*Lawson*' with '*Mountain Sweet*' and created a large dark-skinned oblong watermelon with delicious, sweet and fragrant flesh which he named '*Bradford*'. By the 1860s it had become the most important late-season watermelon in the south, and was highly sought after. It was in such high demand that it had to be protected from gangs who would try to steal the fruit from the farmers' fields. At night, people would patrol the patches with guns to ward off potential suitors, and some farmers took to poisoning unmarked fruits and put up 'Pick at your own risk' notices. An 1884 article read 'At Salem, Ohio, five men have died from eating watermelons that had been drugged', and in 1900 'six boys were poisoned and killed in a watermelon patch in Bluffdale, Texas'. It wasn't only the potential thieves that died, sometimes the farmers themselves forgot which fruit they had doctored and became victims themselves, as a county newspaper in Kansas reported: '1893. Neal Pinyerd. Accidentally killed in a watermelon patch near Denton, in August'. The deterrents did not stop there, and as America became electrified in the 1880s so did the choice watermelons, giving rogue pickers a shock that, if they survived, they would not want to experience again. It is suggested at this time that more people died in watermelon fields than in any other area of agriculture, apart from cattle rustling and horse stealing.

Six generations on, the 'Bradford' watermelon was no longer a commercial variety, mainly due the introduction of industrial farming in the 1920s, and also due to the fact that it had a thin rind, which made it unsuitable for shipping, particularly travelling long distances in the new railway freight carriages. It was not being grown by anybody and was thought lost. In 1997, Bradford's great grandson, Nat Bradford, was pursuing a career in architecture when he read a copy of *Field and Garden Vegetables of America* by Fearing Burr from 1863, and in the watermelon section the 'Bradford' was listed as being 'highly prized' and the 'best' variety. This inspired Nat to quit his job and return to the family farm in Sumter and try to grow watermelons again. Fortunately, seeds had been kept by successive Bradford generations of farmers on this land, which allowed Nat to bring the 'Bradford' back. To make the farm sustainable none of the watermelon is wasted, and Nat has diversified into producing watermelon rind pickle (made to his grandmother's recipe), molasses, and even watermelon brandy. Seeds can now be bought for growers to try at home, though sadly their long season and heat requirements rule them out for UK growers, but it is perhaps the greatest and most romantic heritage story there is, and demonstrates the necessity and importance of growing and saving the seed of old varieties.

The Quest to Grow Watermelons in Cold Climates

We are now able to grow watermelons far away from their ideal climate, and this is thanks to the work of plant breeders, both amateur and professional. Developing a new variety takes time, patience and skill. There are some short season watermelons whose breeding stories should be told.

Glenn Drowns was gardening from a very young age in the foothills of Blacktail Mountain in Idaho, and he looked forward to eating watermelon each year. He was desperate to grow watermelons at his home but the climate, with summer average night-time temperatures of 5 to 10°C, was in no way suitable for the varieties available for cultivation. So, as a teenager, he set out to breed his own by crossing a variety of different heritage types to produce a plant that would not only survive but thrive and reliably crop in cold and short-season areas. After ten years he had stabilised a very dark-skinned watermelon with red flesh that would produce every year, and he named it '*Blacktail Mountain*'. He offered it to the Seed Savers Exchange in 1983 and it became commercially available in 1994. Glenn's watermelon is still considered by many growers the number one choice for cold climates and a great starting point for gardeners new to growing watermelons.

Albert F. Yeager was born in 1892 and worked extensively from his post at the North Dakota Agricultural College on breeding hardy vegetables and fruits for growing in the northern regions of the US.

He later joined the University of New Hampshire, where his early work was on trying to breed small 'midget' watermelons suited to easier public consumption. His success came in 1950 when he introduced the '*New Hampshire Midget*' and in 1951 it was awarded a gold medal by the All-American Selections (ALS). Yeager was then joined by botanist Elwyn Meader and together they went to work on creating another watermelon variety superior to '*New Hampshire Midget*'. This was a challenge until someone sent them seeds of an early season heritage variety from Oklahoma called '*Pumpkin Rind*'. They went on to cross this with Yeager's original watermelon and eventually created a variety on compact vines that would crop anywhere with 70 frost-free days. The quirk of this new watermelon was that it had a built-in ripeness indicator, as soon as the rind turned from green to yellow, it was ready to harvest. They named it '*Golden Midget*' and it was made available to growers in 1959. It is an excellent, reliable and compact watermelon which is recommended for new short-season growers and those with an interest in heritage varieties.

'Howden' pumpkin

THE STORY OF THE SQUASH

Origin

Pumpkins, patty pans, hubbards, courgettes and marrows are all part of the squash family, which is generally divided into winter squashes (the ones which form a hard skin and are stored all winter) and summer squashes (which are eaten young and fresh). Their ancestors originated in Central America and were grown in Mexico as early as 5,000 to 7,000 BC. They have been an integral part of the *Día de los Muertos* (Day of the Dead) celebrations since Aztec times. When the Spanish conquerors brought sugar cane and their sugar making equipment the locals used it to slow-cook winter squash with spices and make a traditional dessert called Calabaza en Tacha.

By 2700 BC, squash had spread into North America, where they were being grown and shared by Native American tribes. It is believed that Christopher Columbus was part of the first group of Europeans to see a pumpkin patch in Cuba in 1492; he took seeds back and introduced pumpkins to Europe. They were first pictured in Europe in the prayer book of Anne de Bretagne in the early 1500s. They then spread throughout Southern Europe and onwards including into Asia, most likely via the well-established Silk Road trading route. In the 1800s the zucchini (or courgette) was bred near

Milan. A huge variety of winter and summer squashes have been developed which have become very adaptable growers and are now cultivated on all continents of the world apart from Antarctica.

HALLOWE'EN: WARDING OFF EVIL SPIRITS WITH A TURNIP OR A PUMPKIN?

The pumpkin has become the symbol of Hallowe'en but the tradition has Celtic origins going back 2,000 years. The Celts, living mostly in what is now Ireland, but also in other parts of the UK and northern France, marked two major events in the annual calendar with festivals. One was *Beltane*, which celebrated the end of the harsh winter and the start of spring, and *Samhain*, held on the 31st October/1st November, which marked the onset of the cold, dark winter often associated with death. At these times, particularly at *Samhain*, they believed that the boundary between the living and dead worlds became blurred, and that it was a vulnerable time. To ensure a safe winter and ward off evil and the return of the dead, they carved scary faces, not into pumpkins (which they did not know existed), but into the root vegetables they grew, such as beetroots and turnips.

Christianity had made its way to Ireland by the ninth century and the traditions and celebrations began to merge and be replaced. Eventually the Church introduced All Souls' Day to honour the dead, which some people believe was an attempt to replace an important Celtic day with a Christian one. It was celebrated in a similar way to *Samhain* with bonfires and rituals to ward off evil spirits, and was known as All-Hallows. The night before, the 31st, the most important night of *Samhain*, became known as All-Hallows Eve, and then by contraction Hallowe'en. When Irish immigrants were fleeing to America to escape the potato famine in the nineteenth century they introduced the Hallowe'en tradition to North America, where squashes were being grown in abundance. The root vegetables were eventually replaced by the larger, orange and easier to carve pumpkin.

WORLD RECORD PUMPKINS AND THE £1,250 SEED

Growing giant pumpkins for competition is a dedicated business full of secret techniques, watering and feeding regimes, the ultimate quest being to hold the world record for the heaviest pumpkin. The history of giant pumpkin competitions can be traced back to the World Fair held in Chicago in 1893, where these large squashes were a curiosity. By 1900, competitions for the largest pumpkin were held at the World Fair in Paris, the winner weighing in at just over 180 kg (400 lb). The weights stayed relatively low until Howard Dill from Nova Scotia bred *Atlantic Giant* in 1979, which topped the scales at 199 kg (438 lb). Since then, every world record holder has been of this variety.

The World Championship Pumpkin Weigh-Off is held in Half Moon Bay, California, every October and offers sizeable prize money with the winner being paid $9 per pound of pumpkin, second prize $3,000 and third place $2,500. If the world record is broken at the event, then $30,000 is up for grabs. The 2020 winner received $16,450. This long-standing interest of competitive growing across North America has been reflected with growers from Canada and the US dominating the previous world record holders. However, in recent years the record has been broken by European gardeners. The current world record pumpkin, weighing in at 1,226 kg (2,702 lb) was grown by Stefano Cutrupi in Italy.

The potential financial rewards don't end with the competitions, as the seed from the winning pumpkins are heavily sought after by

Squashes

other growers on their quest to hold the world record. Seeds from Travis Gienger's 2020 Half Moon winner have sold for $100 each, and UK seed company Thompson & Morgan paid £1250 at auction for a single seed of the previous world record holder from Belgium. Not every grower carries this quest for financial reward; many seeds from champions are donated to pumpkin growing associations across North America for annual auctions. The funds raised help to support the organisations to operate, run shows and offer prize money for future winners, which keeps the competitions flourishing and the history alive.

'*Crystal Lemon*' cucumber

THE STORY OF THE CUCUMBER

ORIGIN

Native to India, cucumbers, *Cucumis sativus*, have been in cultivation for at least 3,000 years, with evidence that the Egyptians were growing them freely. They are mentioned in the Bible, Numbers 11:5: 'We remember the fish we ate in Egypt at no cost – also the cucumbers, melons, leeks, onions and garlic', and Egyptian pottery models of cucumbers have been dated to 1850-1700 BC. The initial cucumbers will most probably have been bitter, a problem that can persist in some heritage varieties today, but which would have been gradually bred out by skilled gardeners. They were introduced to China before making their way to Europe by the Greeks, and then the Romans. Pliny the Elder reported that Emperor Tiberius demanded a cucumber on his dining table every day of the year. To meet this demand, fruit needed to be produced in winter and spring, and this required the creation of some of the first forcing houses, several of which were mounted on wheels so they could be moved around the garden for maximum sunlight in winter. However, there is debate among historians that the cucumbers Tiberius so favoured were the elongated types of melon, *Cucumis melo*, rather than *Cucumis sativus*.

Charlemagne was said to be growing cucumbers in Italy in the eighth and ninth centuries, and they were believed to be a favourite of Catherine of Aragon, Henry VIII's first wife. Christopher Columbus' exploration of the New World took cucumbers to Haiti in 1494, and throughout the 1500s European explorers, trappers and hunters traded with Native Americans across North America. The Mandan and Abenaki tribes of the Great Plains were growing them along with other introduced crops such as beans, corn and squash.

However, by the eighteenth century, the enthusiasm for cucumbers had waned significantly as people began to be suspicious of them, thinking it was dangerous to eat vegetables which were not cooked, something the cucumber does not lend itself to. By the nineteenth century it was back on the menu and its popularity increased rapidly, helped in the US by Heinz adding pickled cucumbers to its range in 1876. Cucumbers were also much beloved by gardeners on Victorian estates in Britain, who were responsible for many new varieties.

The Straightest Cucumber: A Victorian Gardener's Obsession

The cucumbers which were historically grown in the UK needed to be cultivated in greenhouses, and they produced bitter fruits when the pollen from the male flowers was transferred to the female ones. To produce the best quality required skill and dedication. To many Victorians with large walled gardens attached to big estates, growing the highest quality cucumber was an obsession, with glasshouses dedicated solely to the fruit. One result of this infatuation was the breeding of the '*Telegraph Improved*' variety, which became the number one choice for any respectable head gardener. It was celebrated for producing a long, thin-skinned and tender cucumber. The ultimate reward, as with melons, was to win awards at the premier gardening shows. This was regarded as a seal of approval, not just for the gardener but the owner of the estate on which it was grown. Many gardeners of the time bred their versions of the '*Telegraph Improved*' and named them after themselves, members of the royal family or their employees. These names could then be seen on the show bench by the public and by neighbouring estate owners, with the rights of the best being sold off to the biggest seed suppliers of the day. '*Rollinson's Telegraph Improved*' is one such variety still available today. It was big business, and some unscrupulous seed suppliers would sell seeds of the same variety but give them a different name to attract the buyer. It required an act of parliament to put an end to such behaviour.

To win a first-class prize at horticultural shows required uniform growth along the length of the cucumber, and gardeners across the country tried to get theirs to be the straightest. George Stephenson, the Victorian civil engineer and 'father of the railway', was also a very keen fruit grower, taking particular pride in his cucumbers. While living at Tapton House in Derbyshire he used his inventor's skills to create the ultimate cucumber straightener. He designed an elongated glass tube which he had made at his Newcastle steam engine factory. The glass was placed over a young fruit which then developed inside the tube and therefore could only grow straight. This method was not without risk – if the cucumber was not keenly observed daily it could quickly grow too wide and become stuck inside the glass. So popular was this invention that an 1848 advert in the *Gardeners' Chronicle and Agricultural Gazette* offered a range of different size straighteners from 12 to 24 inches. Sadly, this method became too expensive as it required more labour than was available, especially after the First World War, and it fell out of favour. However, straight cucumbers still remain the most desirable today, as they are more efficient to pack and transport, and easier to use in the kitchen.

Cantaloupe melon

MELONS AND WATERMELONS IN THE GARDEN

Even though melons and watermelons belong to a different genus the growing conditions are very similar so they are described together in this section.

BOTANICAL INFORMATION

Melons and watermelons are from the same family, *Cucurbitaceae*, but are from a different genus: melons belonging to *Cucumis melo* and watermelons being *Citrullus lanatus*. Melons have a great variety of fruit sizes, shapes and appearances, which over the years has resulted in many attempts at classification. This has not been helped by the ease with which melons cross and produce new varieties. Pitrat et al (2000) is the most comprehensive and widely-used classification, and breaks down melons into sixteen different cultivar groups. Of these, there are three main groups that gardeners should be familiar with:

Cantalupensis have been historically grown in Europe, and have a ribbed, smooth or warted skin. They can have rough areas on the skin but are not 'netted' (a term derived from their Latin name, which translates as reticulated or marked like a net or network). In general, these are most suited to growing in the

UK, and include varieties such as *'Charentais'*, *'Petis Gris de Rennes'* and *'Ogen'*.

Reticulatus are commonly called musk melons (though in North America they are confusingly referred to as cantaloupes), and are defined by their heavily netted skin. Varieties include *'Blenheim Orange'* and *'Green Nutmeg'*.

Inodorus are known as casaba or winter melons but labelled as honeydew in the supermarkets. They have a hard ribbed skin which is usually yellow or green but can be nearly white. They have no fragrance but are crisp and sweeter than most other melons. They descend from Spain, Turkey and the Middle East, and require a long, hot season to thrive and generate their full sweetness so are therefore difficult to grow in the UK. If they are your favourite melons to eat then *'Collective Farm Woman'* is the best choice for flavour, and *'Giallo d'Inverno'* is a good option if you want a traditional looking casaba melon. Another of the groups to note is the Ameri, which includes the *'Ananas'* variety which is an excellent melon to grow and eat.

Nutritional Benefits

Melons are a good source of dietary fibre. They also contain vitamin C, which helps maintain a healthy immune system; vitamin B, which helps to form red blood cells, improve brain function and release energy from foods; potassium, which is important for heart health and has been linked to reducing blood pressure; and copper, which aids skin cell regeneration. Watermelons contain lycopene, which is a powerful antioxidant found in red-coloured fruit and vegetables. The darker the red the more lycopene it contains.

Antioxidants help prevent cell damage and may prevent several types of cancer.

Common Causes of Failure

In most gardening books the cultivation problems section comes at the end. However, the aim of this book is to encourage you to try growing melons, and to try again if you have failed before. Therefore, it is advantageous to highlight some of the major common causes of failure and describe techniques to prevent them. This leads into a section on growing techniques, which aims to offer different ways to cultivate melons in the UK and avoid these problems.

Root Transplant Shock

All cucurbits dislike root disturbance but melons and watermelons are the worst affected. They can stop growing for a prolonged period, which is time you generally do not have when trying to get a good crop of melons in the UK climate. In the worst-case scenario, but sadly not at all rare, the plant can die from root shock. The sure signs are wilting within the first day or two, and/or very slow or no growth. If you are unsure whether the plant is growing, measure a new leaf with a ruler, make a note of the width of the leaf and check it again over the next couple of days. If the weather is warm and sunny there should be a noticeable increase in size. If any of these symptoms of root shock are noticed, give it a few days of settled warm weather, and if it does not improve or gets worse, replace it.

Fortunately, there are some techniques which can be used to avoid this. Direct sowing into the ground is not really an option with the short and unreliable UK growing season. Therefore, the only option is to sow into pots, then grow on and plant out. Some people will sow seed into trays and prick out as soon as the first seed leaves have developed. This can work but is to be avoided where possible. Any pricking out risks disturbing the roots. Seed should be sown into pots, either one or two seeds, whichever you decide on (see Propagation section, below), into 7 or 8 cm diameter plastic pots. Grow the plants on until they produce their fourth true leaf (four leaves after the two seed leaves). The fourth leaf does not have to be full size, just large enough to be recognisable. At this point, the plant will have produced a big enough root ball in this size pot to hold all the compost together. If planted out before the plant has reached this stage there is a risk that when it is taken out of the pot the compost will fall away and expose the roots. This will invariably lead to root shock. Watermelons, which are more vigorous growers, can be planted out at the three-leaf stage if the planting conditions are right and you are eager. If weather conditions and temperatures are not optimal then it is possible to wait until melon plants have five or six true leaves (four or five for watermelons). Any longer than this and the plant can become stunted and fall behind others planted at the correct time.

When it comes to planting, the best technique is to take an empty pot of the same size and use this as a mould to make a planting hole. Place the pot in the compost deep enough to cover roughly half of the pot (the top half of the pot should be protruding from the compost) and then build up the mound of compost up to the rim. The top of the pot should now be level with the surrounding compost, with the compost sloping away to the original pre-planting compost level. Give the compost a good water by pouring the water directly into the pot and allowing it to drain away. Make sure the compost is moist, but not soaking wet. It may also be necessary to gently water the mound around the pot with a fine rose or misting spray, so that the compost is moist and stays in place when the pot-mould is removed. Ideally carry this out a couple of days in advance to allow the now damp soil to warm up. If this is not possible then water with warm water. Gently remove the pot and it should leave the perfect sized hole to match the melon plant root ball. Take the potted plant and place a hand, palm side down, over the top with the fingers split either side of the stem, then gently tip the pot upside down and carefully squeeze the pot and the plant should drop softly into the palm. Take the plant, and as gently as possible guide it into the pre-prepared hole that has been made. Do not firm in. Let it settle naturally. It may be necessary to top up the compost mound to make sure the root ball is covered. The plant can gently be watered in with a small amount of water, depending on when the planting hole was pre-watered.

Some growers are successful in avoiding transplant shock by sowing the seed into biodegradable pots, such as those made from paper fibre and coir. These are then planted, pot included, into the ground and the roots grow through them. This reduces root transplant shock and is arguably more environmentally friendly than plastic. However, the biodegradable pots can easily sit cold and wet when conditions prior to planting are not optimal, which melons greatly dislike. Therefore, they always need to be kept warm, but then they have a habit of drying out quicker than in pots. This is something that you can potentially trial yourself, particularly if you are having transplant shock issues.

STEM ROT (SOFT COLLAR ROT)

Stem rot is a very common cause of failure, particularly in the first few weeks and months of growing. Often, gardeners are used to growing and caring for traditional greenhouse crops such as tomatoes, peppers, aubergines and cucumbers (cucumbers can be victim to stem rot but are not as susceptible as melons and watermelons), which they water liberally with the leaves and stems of the plants getting wet. While this is fine for those listed above, for a melon plant a wet stem, particularly when followed by cooler nights, will quickly spell disaster. Water must be prevented from sitting on the stem from the moment the seedling appears above the compost. At the seedling stage the best way to achieve this is to cover the surface of the compost with vermiculite (perlite is acceptable but not as good as vermiculite, see the Propagation section below for reasons why), and water from the top, using a water bottle with a watering nozzle or a small watering can without the rose attached. Water around the edges of the pot only and well away from the stem, which will ideally be in the centre of the pot. Once the water drains from the bottom of the pot, stop watering and make sure that the pot does not stand in water, which makes the compost too wet and risks stem rot.

When planting the seedlings into their final positions – be that pots, grow bags or into beds – they must be planted on a mound to ensure any water drains away from the stem. The easiest way to achieve this is to use an empty pot the same size as the one the seedling is growing in. Dig a hole about half the depth of the pot, place the pot in, and mound up compost to the rim. Leave the pot in place for a few days, and water into it and gently around the mound to help it set firmly in place. It will have created a sufficient mound to prevent water collecting around the stem and a perfect mould for the plant to gently drop into, hopefully without creating any root shock. Dust all around the mound and where the stem touches the soil with yellow sulphur. This helps to prevent any fungal diseases, lowers the soil pH, and adds trace nutrients. Reapply when this has worked its way into the soil.

Throughout its growing life, ensure that whenever watering keep moisture away from the stem. Initially, after transplanting, the plant will need to be gently watered around the base of the mound to make sure the roots have access to water and are encouraged to grow away from the planting hole. As the plant matures and the roots grow further from the stem, so can the watering, making it easier to prevent the stem getting wet and sitting in damp compost.

Root Rot

Root rot takes place when the roots of the plant sit in cold wet soil for prolonged periods. The risk is obviously higher at the beginning and end of the growing season, but it can happen during unseasonable cold spells if they last long enough. The symptoms are not noticeable at the time the roots are being lost but it quickly shows itself once the weather warms up again, as the plant's leaves wilt in the sun. It can also cause the leaves to turn yellow, and female flowers to be aborted. This is because the plant had developed roots to support its top growth, but has now lost a proportion of them and so can no longer provide moisture to the amount of leaves it has. The plant can and will recover from this if the temperatures stay warm, but the process is slow and can delay flowering and fruiting by weeks rather than days. At the beginning of the season when the plant is small the recovery is quicker, if this happens midseason (e.g. July) then losing two weeks growing time can be the difference between enjoying eating a home-grown melon and thinking about what could have been.

The ideal situation is not to let the soil temperature drop below 10°C. In reality this is harder to achieve than it sounds. Short periods, such as overnight, just below 10°C are acceptable if the weather is warm the next day. During a cold spell of numerous back-to-back days with sub-10°C nights and cold rainy days you might need to take steps to raise the soil temperature. The easiest and most effective way, if you have electricity to your greenhouse or polytunnel, is to run heat cables under the grow bags, pots or the plants planted in the beds. If you do have this luxury then you can easily prevent root rot and force an earlier crop by turning the heating cables on every night below 10ºC, and every day below 15-18ºC. However, most amateur gardeners do not have the facilities to be able do this, so an alternative method is required. Conventional hot-water bottles are excellent at providing heat to grow bags in particular. They should be filled as normal and then placed on the top surface of the grow bags between your two plants (it is not advisable to try and push them under the bag with the plants in place as this risks disturbing the roots), and then covered with bubble wrap to reduce heat loss to the air and direct it to the roots. You may need to do this multiple times a day depending on the temperatures. Some people arrange plastic pop bottles filled with water on the soil and around pots and grow bags. During the day the sun heats up the water in the bottles and it is released slowly overnight. This can help through short cooler overnight periods and generally help raise the temperature over the whole growing season, but it will not be enough to heat the soil through prolonged periods. Paraffin heaters or electric heaters will help to raise the air temperature a few degrees which the plants will appreciate, but it will not provide the direct root heat the plants are looking for. If it is not possible to use any of the above methods then you should focus on growing the varieties listed as cold tolerant, such as '*Minnesota Midget*', '*Blacktail Mountain*', or any of the F1s.

GROWING TECHNIQUES

Melons and watermelons may be from a different genus, but their growing requirements are very similar. They like heat, no, they demand it, particularly at their roots. They grow best and quickest with fewest problems when their roots are baked by the sun. They also require the gardener's dreaded 'moisture retentive but free-draining soil', the most difficult to achieve. There are various ways to help achieve this in the UK climate and it is something the gardeners of Victorian estates refined to produce regular crops of melon, even out of season.

The Victorians grew them in glasshouses – often dedicated to the purpose – that were heated with hot water pipes powered by coal-fired boilers tended by large numbers of gardening staff. While we do not all have that luxury what we can do is recognise, copy and adapt their main growing method in our own greenhouses and polytunnels. What the Victorians did was to raise the root zone off the ground to around waist height, originally on crates used to transport lilies, and then onto purpose-built staging. This was a metal mesh rack supported by bricks, on which old grass turfs from the estate grounds were stacked in mounds, with the melons planted in the peak of those mounds and trained up along the glass with the fruits supported by nets. The wire rack allowed the growing medium to be very free draining and put the roots in direct sunlight, where they want to be. The heating helped to guarantee a crop and allowed them to be forced to fruit out of season.

To provide the heat and protection melons and watermelons need, they should be grown in a greenhouse or polytunnel. If you do not have either and cannot obtain one (you will never regret owning a greenhouse or polytunnel), then good results can also be obtained on a hot bed or by planting in ground covered with black plastic mulch (both described in detail later in this section), provided they can be covered at the beginning and end of the season, as well as during unfavourable weather.

Soil pH

Both melons and watermelons prefer a slightly acid soil, ideally between pH 6.0 and 6.5 but will grow adequately up to 7.0 (neutral), which is the pH value of most bought in compost. The pH of the compost or soil is important as it affects the ability of the plant to take up nutrients. If growing direct in the ground, you should aim to take a pH test of your soil using a bought pH test or a pH soil meter. If you cannot or you forget to test the compost you have purchased, then if you assume it is pH 7.0 you will not go far wrong. The easiest way to lower your pH into the preferred zone of the melon is by applying a good dusting of yellow sulphur to the surface of the compost. This is readily available from garden centres and it not only gently reduces the pH, it adds sulphur which is an important nutrient for photosynthesis and protein production, and also helps to prevent stem rot. Using yellow sulphur is one of the key steps that should significantly increase your chances of success.

Where possible, only water using rainwater. UK water regulations state that tap water should have a pH between 6.5 and 9.5 and is typically above neutral (7.0) and therefore alkaline. While rainwater is fortunately not as acid as it used to be, it still generally has a pH lower than tap water. If you are in doubt, check it with a pH test.

Propagation

The first rule is to sow early, aim for mid-April. In warmer climates and longer season areas, gardeners have the option of sowing direct into the ground as soon as the risk of frost and weather conditions are right. In the UK we don't have that luxury, so there is no option but to sow, and grow on, in pots before planting out. By sowing early, you are stealing time on the season by gaining 4 to 6 weeks growth before planting out, which brings forward the flowering – and most importantly the fruit ripening – into the warmer months of August and September. It is much easier to steal time at the beginning of the season, when light is increasing daily and there are some hot days in the sun. By the second week of October temperatures don't get hot enough or for long enough to sustain ripening. You are fighting a losing battle. To be able to start early you are going to need some heat and a place to keep plants frost free until the middle of May in a good year, or the beginning of June in a year with a cold spring.

The second rule is to grow spare plants, at least one per variety you are growing. The common problems section will have given you a feel for why this is necessary, mainly so you have a replacement should you suffer losses due to transplant shock. If you do not end up requiring the spares, enjoy your success and give them to friends to try rather than composting them.

Even though the seeds of melons and watermelons are smaller, they should be sown on their side, as with all cucurbits. If they are sown flat there is a risk of water gathering on them in the soil and the seeds rotting before they germinate. The compost should be good quality multi-purpose (peat-free provides excellent results) with added drainage. Perlite is good for this, better than horticultural grit which is heavier and does not aerate the soil like perlite does. About a quarter to a third of this should make up the total planting mix.

Sow two seeds on their side into a 7 or 8 cm pot and cover with compost to a depth the same size as the seed (imagine another seed is on top of the seed you are sowing). Cover the surface with a good layer of vermiculite, enough so no soil is visible, to help prevent damping off and stem rot. You can use perlite for this, but vermiculite dries out and provides an indication of when the plant needs watering. This can be difficult to determine with perlite as it always remains dry, even when the compost is saturated. Give them a gentle water from the top so you are confident the water has soaked as far as the seed. They do not need to be completely saturated, just evenly moist. Do not leave them sitting in water, or water them by standing them in a tray of water at any stage. This is a recipe for seed or stem rot.

Place the pots in a heated propagator which provides bottom heat. If you do not have a heated propagator, on top of a radiator or on a sunny windowsill would be adequate but not ideal. What they need for quick reliable germination is a continuous bottom heat of 20°C or higher, at which temperature, with fresh seed, they will be up and visible within a week. They will germinate even quicker at 30°C. Watermelons have a thicker seed coat so take longer to germinate. To speed this up they can be pre-soaked in a bowl of warm water overnight. Watermelons have a higher optimum germination temperature of just above 30°C, but with the pre-soak they will germinate fine in a propagator at 20°C, which is what most standard heated propagators are set to operate around.

If the seeds are to be germinated on a windowsill or radiator, then the pots need to be placed into an unheated propagator (a tray with a clear removable plastic lid), or if you do not have one, a clear sandwich bag will suffice. The aim of the cover is to maintain humidity and prevent regular drying out of the compost, which can create erratic germination. Remove the bag during the day once seeds have germinated and place in good light. Replace the bag at night until the plants have grown two true leaves. If they are to be grown on indoors and they cannot be placed in a greenhouse during warm sunny days, they need rotating regularly to prevent the seedlings pulling and leaning towards the light. If you do not do this it can result in etiolated (leggy) seedlings with a long stem before the first leaves, which is prone to falling over or snapping. Thin stems are also vulnerable to stem rot.

If both seeds in the pot germinate then one of them needs to be removed. Choose the smallest or weakest and snip the stem at soil level with a pair of scissors. Do not be tempted to pull out the seedling as it risks disturbing the roots of the one you wish to keep.

If you cannot bring yourself to dispose of a seedling or have rare or a small number of seeds, then it is best to germinate them using damp paper towels or kitchen roll. A small container with a lid or a resealable sandwich bag is required. Take two sheets of kitchen roll and get them thoroughly damp. If using a container then line the bottom with one sheet of kitchen roll, place the seeds apart from each other and then cover with the remaining kitchen roll and seal with the lid. If using a sandwich bag, line each side of the bag with kitchen roll, with the seeds placed between them, and seal. Put these in your propagator or on top of the radiator. With good fresh seed germination should take place in one to two days under consistent heat. The white root will emerge from the seed coat first. At this point you know the seed is viable and has germinated, and it can

Germinating seed in kitchen roll

Germinated seed

be transferred to a pot to grow on. Fill the pot with compost and gently take the germinated seed (a small piece of thin card is useful for sliding under and lifting the seed) and place it on the compost, taking care not to damage the root. Lightly cover with compost and finish with a layer of vermiculite. Place it back in your chosen propagator to germinate fully.

Once the seeds have germinated and the plants have produced their two seed leaves (cotyledons) keep them on the heat. On sunny warm days turn off the heat, remove the propagator lid (or sandwich bag) and then put the lid and heat back on overnight. If the propagator is inside, move them to the greenhouse on sunny days then back inside on the heat at night. This may seem like a lot of work but you will be rewarded with good, stout and well-developed plants.

Once they have reached the stage of four or five true leaves (three or four for watermelons) then they are ready for planting in their final growing position. See the section Root Transplant Shock above for techniques on how to do this. Do not be tempted to pot on into a larger container to grow on, as this creates another opportunity for root disturbance which the plant will not appreciate.

MELONS & OTHER CUCURBITS

Grow Bags

The advantage of grow bags is that they distribute the roots over a shallow wide area which can gain maximum sunlight and heat across the full root zone. The plastic bags are excellent at absorbing heat from the sun and transferring it to the compost while retaining moisture, as only a small amount of the growing medium (at the planting holes) is directly exposed to the sun. The design of the bag also allows heat to be provided to the compost in unseasonable weather or on sub-10°C nights. This is easily achieved by placing a standard hot-water bottle on the centre of the bag. Cover the top side of the bottle with bubble wrap to increase the amount of heat that goes into the compost rather than being lost to the atmosphere.

Purchase the best quality grow bag you can (excellent results can equally be obtained with peat-free grow bags), place them in full sun and raise them up to waist height or as high as you can, by making your own homemade Victorian-style wire racks placed on bricks or cement blocks, or putting them on greenhouse staging. Raise the bags off the staging using bricks or pieces of wood, or make a wooden frame, as this will enable the bags to drain off any excess water and stop them standing in the puddles that drain out, avoiding the risk of root rot.

A standard size grow bag will accommodate two melon plants, each planted a third of the way from the end edges of the bag. The new extra-large grow bags will accommodate three plants. Follow the grow bag instructions, but all bags should first be given a good shake to loosen, open up and evenly distribute the compost before planting. Cut out a square of the plastic about twice as big as the pot (most grow bags have useful cut-out markings printed on the bag), remove a hole about half the depth of the pot size you have your young melon plant in. Build up a mound around the plastic pot with fresh compost to allow water to be kept away from the stem. Follow the planting instructions as described in the Root Transplant Shock section earlier. A hole should be cut in the middle for a plastic plant pot to be sunk 1 to 2 cm deep into the compost for watering. Be careful when watering as most grow bags contain compost which is designed to hold onto moisture rather than dry out quickly, and this can easily lead to overwatering issues and root rot, particularly if there is a cold spell during the growing season. Water less regularly than you would for tomatoes, and check the compost regularly. If the compost feels moist, do not water.

POTS AND OTHER CONTAINERS

When it comes to pots, black plastic is your friend. As much as terracotta or a coloured glazed pot wins in the looks stakes, it is substance over style that wins when it comes to growing melons. What black plastic offers is a thin wall which absorbs the most heat and readily transfers it to the compost, which the melons will appreciate.

Use a good quality multi-purpose or peat-free compost with a handful of organic slow-release fertiliser (such as chicken manure pellets or fish, blood and bone) mixed in. Add some perlite if you have it for improved drainage, less than is necessary for seeds, but the roots will appreciate anything up to a third of the total volume. Raise the pots off the ground and place in full sun, on staging if you have it, if not then on bricks or on top of a sturdy upturned pot. A brick or flagged floor will absorb the heat during the day and release it back during the night as temperatures cool, so you can place your pots on them if you choose. It is important that the pot is raised off whichever surface you choose, by using bricks or pieces of wood, as this will prevent the plants sitting in pools of water, which significantly increases the chances of root rot.

MELONS & OTHER CUCURBITS

A pot size of 28 cm (11 in) in diameter (measured across the top and often called a 10 litre pot) is ideal for one plant, and a few centimetres bigger will be fine but avoid going smaller. Some people prefer to cultivate three plants in one pot and have had good success in doing so by growing them up a support system. For this you will need a pot 40 to 50 cm (16 to 20 in) in diameter (30 to 40 litre).

The main advantage the black pot has over the grow bag is that as the melons grow the leaves can shade the surface of the grow bag and prevent the roots being heated up to the same degree as pots, which have a greater vertical surface area that the leaves do not shade. The only disadvantage of growing in a pot is that should you get an unseasonable cold spell they are difficult to add heat to, unlike grow bags. There is potential to place a hot-water bottle under the pot, but it would be difficult to put one on the surface without damaging the plant. These are, of course, minor details but the more you can stack in your favour the greater your chances of success will be. Black plastic pots are the best container method for beginners, as the compost can be mixed to specific requirements, and watering is easier to manage.

Some people grow melons in the bags designed for growing potatoes or in a strong plastic bag, such as an old compost bag. As they are made from plastic and are thin but strong, they allow the sun to heat up the soil quickly and keep it warm. If you try this method you need to cut or roll the bags down to one third for a standard compost bag, or a half for the potato growing bag. Melons do not require the depth of a full bag, as it runs the risk of creating cold damp areas in the bag that the sun cannot get to and warm up, a situation the roots will not thank you for. It is important to make sure there are enough drainage holes, and you must also raise them off the surface on bricks or pieces of wood to ensure free drainage.

Melons can be successfully grown in old tyres. The advantage of this is that the black rubber is excellent at absorbing and retaining heat from the sun. However, there are concerns regarding the release of chemicals into the soil as the tyre breaks down. If you choose this method then line the tyres with an old compost bag to prevent direct contact with the compost, place them on ground that has been turned over or loosened and is weed free, and fill with good quality compost. They can support two plants if necessary (stick to one plant for watermelons) as the roots will make their way into the soil you have prepared below the tyre.

WATERMELONS IN CONTAINERS

Watermelons are vigorous growers that can grow vines three metres or more in length in multiple directions, and they root widely. Therefore, not all of them are ideally suited for growing in containers the way melons are. If this is the method you prefer, or it is your only option, you should choose the smaller fruited varieties such as *Little Darling*, *Petite Yellow* or *Golden Midget*. If you can accommodate grow bags then the 'icebox' varieties (i.e. those small enough to fit in your fridge) such as *Sugar Baby* and *Champagne* should be successful with two plants per bag, but limit them to one fruit per plant for maximum size and flavour. Keep them consistently moist (not waterlogged) and well fed.

GROWING IN BEDS UNDERCOVER

Melons and watermelons can be successfully grown in beds in greenhouses or polytunnels. While a lot of people have enjoyed success this way it is not the preferable method for a reliable crop or for trying out a wide range of varieties. The major disadvantages are that as the soil is at or close to ground level it does not offer the level of drainage required, and it is also difficult to warm it up and have it retain that heat. The only realistic way to add additional heat when required is to run heat cables in the soil under the plants. If this is the way you wish to grow them there are couple of tricks you can do to shift the odds in your favour.

Raise the soil into mounds or ridges and plant into the top of them. The mounds improve drainage dramatically and they offer a bank of soil which faces the sun and therefore gets more heat than if the soil was level. If you have grown melons or any of the cucurbit family in the bed the previous year, replace the soil and then prepare it by digging it over and incorporating some well-rotted manure and organic fertiliser. Build the mounds up so they are 30 to 45 cm (12 to 18 in) high and 60 cm (24 in) wide. If you are planting multiple melons, make this into a long ridge rather than individual mounds. Plant approximately 40 cm (16 in) apart and train the plants vertically or allow to scramble over the ground.

You can increase the heat absorption of the compost even further by covering the mounds or ridges with black plastic and planting

Watermelons growing in polytunnels

through it. Black weed-proof membrane or black plastic sheets work well for this (see the following section for more details). It also prevents any weeds from growing.

Growing Melons and Watermelons Outside

Growing outside is very much possible in the UK if a few adjustments are made. It is a good option for watermelons, which put on a lot of growth in multiple directions and are therefore difficult to train vertically or grow in pots, but it can also work equally well for melons.

The trick for success outside is to be able to increase the temperature and retain it in the soil. There are two ways to achieve this and ideally you should use both. The first – and this is essential – is to cover the ground with black plastic or weed-proof membrane. Black plastic with a gauge of 500 / 125 mu is ideal, as it is not too thick but captures the sun's heat and warms the soil significantly. The other option is heavy duty woven weed control fabric made from plastic, not the lightweight non-woven version which doesn't absorb enough heat. The woven fabric will warm the soil but not quite as much as black plastic. However, it does let moisture through, whereas black plastic does not. If you use plastic then holes will need to be made in it for watering. If you can water regularly (daily in hot spells) then black plastic is preferred, due to how well it heats the soil and allows you to control the water the plant receives. If getting to the melons for regular watering is an issue, then woven weed-proof membrane will allow any rainfall through it.

The second step is to be able to cover the plants with clear plastic at the beginning and end of the growing season, and through any cold and rainy spells. The best material for this is polytunnel plastic which can be bought by the metre, or if you are lucky you may be able to source some off-cuts from a polytunnel installation. To achieve this, it is necessary to create a mini polytunnel structure to support the plastic sheet and prevent it sitting on the plants and damaging them. The best way to do this is to install some low half circle supports made from MDPE water pipe, or similar material. Bamboo canes are not strong enough and have the potential to break when being forced into a curve. Aim for the supports to be approximately 60 cm (24 in) high at the apex, and it may need three, four or five of them (depending on the size of the growing area) running parallel along the bed. Cut the pipe to the length you need to create a half circle over your growing area then push short bamboo canes (30 to 45 cm or 12 to 18 in long) into the ground at the edge of the growing area and thread the water pipe onto the bamboo canes to create a half circle. The canes will keep the water pipe rigid and prevent it being blown away, which it would do if the lengths of pipe were simply pushed into the soil. Lay the plastic cover over the pipe structures, making sure it does not rest on the plants, and hold down the edges of the plastic with stones or bricks. During the day, always leave the ends of this mini tunnel open to allow air movement. Cold, damp and stagnant air will cause plants to rot quickly. As soon as the sun comes out, take off the plastic to prevent overheating. Early in the season it is often necessary to re-cover overnight and remove again in the morning. This may seem like a lot of effort, but you will be rewarded with stronger plants that flower and fruit earlier.

Start with a bed of soil that has not had cucurbits growing in it the previous year and has been improved over the winter or early spring with a good amount of added compost.

Ideally, the ground should be free draining, if you are on clay soil which holds onto moisture, then create raised beds to improve drainage. These can be constructed from wood, metal, plastic or bricks, and should be 10 to 30 cm (4 to 12 in) high and filled with good quality compost. If you cannot create raised beds then make mounds or ridges from the compost (as described in the Growing in Beds Undercover section). Try not to walk on the soil, or do so as little as possible, as melons and watermelons are shallow rooted and do not like soil compaction.

Peg or weigh down the black plastic or weed-proof membrane at least a month before you are ready to plant out, around mid-April for planting at the end of May. This will prevent any weeds growing but more importantly it will warm up the soil so the plants can get off to a flying start.

When the weather has warmed up sufficiently to produce regular night-time temperatures of above 10°C – in a good year this can be the end of May, in a not so good one the middle of June – then they are ready for planting out. Each plant should be grown 1.5 to 2 m apart, and squares be cut out of the fabric as planting holes. Use the technique described earlier to prevent stem rot by planting in a small mound, and then dust with yellow sulphur. If you are using black plastic then watering holes will need to be made. Do this by placing a plastic pot approximately 15 to 20 cm (6 to 8 in) from the planting hole, one either side for even watering. Cut around the plastic pot, take out a small amount of soil and sink the pot into the hole. Initially, until the plant is established, you will need to gently water into the planting holes, but you must avoid getting any water onto the stem. Once the plant is established, watering and feeding is done by pouring directly into the plastic pots you have put in place. The water will soak in the soil and the roots will quickly go in search of it. If you are using the weed-proof membrane, water can be applied straight to this as it will soak through the membrane. If you have the option of using a soaker hose then these should be run underneath the plastic or membrane.

If the site is regularly exposed to cold winds then erecting a wind barrier around the melon bed – or at least on the side of the prevailing wind – will be greatly beneficial. This does not need to be very tall, a metre or a little less in height will do, nor does it need to be a permanent structure. Sheets of polycarbonate or fabric sheeting fixed in place with stakes would be enough to buffer the wind and prevent cooling of the plants, and more importantly the soil.

Growing in a Cold Frame or Hot Bed

If you have a cold frame then this can be the perfect place to grow melons. Due to their small size, cold frames do not get as hot or retain heat as polytunnels or greenhouses do, but they offer the ability to cover the plant early in the season and during cold spells. Make sure the soil is free draining, and if it isn't then either dig it out and replace it with compost, or if the cold frame is of reasonable depth half fill it with compost. If possible, cover the surface of compost in the frame with black plastic or woven weed membrane and they will grow even better. Put this cover in place and keep the lid closed for at least two weeks before planting to warm up the compost. Plant into the middle of the frame using the mound method explained earlier and dust with yellow sulphur. Remember to cut a hole and sink in a small plant pot for watering. Once the plant has produced five true leaves, pinch out the growing point (this is the process of removing the very end of a stem after a leaf, or pair of leaves, where a new shoot is developing. This is very soft young growth which can easily be removed by pinching the shoot between the nails of your thumb and finger. The purpose of doing this is to divert energy away from the growing point to other areas of the plant). This will also encourage side shoots, of which the four strongest should be selected, pinching out any others which grow. Train each of the four shoots to the corner of the cold frame and pinch out their growing point when they reach the side of the frame, this will encourage sub-laterals which will produce most of

Growing squash and melon in a hot bed

the flowers. Aim to grow no more than one fruit on each of the four side shoots, otherwise the plant will produce small fruit with poor flavour. Early in the season, when the days are not sunny, it is best to close the lid in the day, and overnight where possible throughout the year. As there is significant danger of overheating and scorching on sunny days when the cover is closed, leave it open to give the foliage ventilation. This will also aid pollination and prevent fungal diseases developing.

A cold frame with a depth of 50 cm (20 in) or more can be turned into a hot bed. If a cold frame is not available then one can be constructed from bricks, concrete blocks or wood. A hot bed has a layer of fresh, un-rotted organic material, underneath a layer of compost. As bacteria and fungi break down the organic material they give off heat, which rises into the soil above it. This will provide extra heat to the roots of your melons and provide a readily available supply of nutrients.

MELONS & OTHER CUCURBITS

If you are constructing your own, then aim for a minimum depth of approximately 50 cm (20 in), though you can build it higher if you wish, and ideally it should be two metres wide in both directions. The hot layer should make up two-thirds of the depth i.e. if the depth is 50 cm (20 in) then the hot layer will fill the bottom 20 cm (8 in), with 10 cm (4 in) of compost placed on top, leaving 20 cm (8 in) for the melon to grow under the cover. The hot layer can contain un-rotted horse manure, wood chips, grass cuttings or wet leaves, ideally a mix of at least two of these, with fresh manure being the best. Cover this with a layer of compost and then add the plastic mulch (plastic sheeting). Do not be tempted to plant straight into the hot layer as the heat can burn the roots. If possible, cover the self-constructed hot bed with clear plastic or glass, like a cold frame, and remove it on warm sunny days and when the plants are in flower. Vigorous plants can grow up to touch the cover – if this happens then remove the cover permanently to prevent scorching and causing other damage to the leaves.

Training Vertically

Melons and watermelons have evolved to grow as vines that trail in multiple directions along the ground, eventually covering anything from 1.5 to 3 metres or more, with watermelons being the most vigorous. For most people, space in a greenhouse or polytunnel is in demand so the best space saving way to grow them is vertically. This isn't really an option for watermelons other than the icebox types with small fruit, as it is difficult to support the weight of them. If you want to grow the larger varieties, then the best method is along the ground using black plastic mulch.

You might read some information that says the central leader should be grown vertically up a cane, and that a shoot on each side should be trained laterally every 30 cm (12 in). However, melons are irregular growers and it is very difficult to get them to comply with such structured training. Unless you want to be removing side shoots from the main stem regularly then you need to accept this is not going to happen. It is also not advisable to create frequent wounds along the main stem, as this increases the chance of bacterial or fungal diseases.

If multiple plants are to be grown side by side, either in grow bags or pots, then a frame made from bamboo canes and wire provides a sturdy support if it is attached to the greenhouse or polytunnel structure. Melons can grow up to two metres (6 ft) tall, so you need to be able to accommodate this height in a straight line to the roof, or be able to train them at an angle once they meet the pitch of the roof. Construct the frame in advance of planting so you are not pushing the canes through and damaging the roots of your newly growing plants. Ideally, the frame should be 30 to 40 cm (12 to 16 in) from the glass or plastic (though this is not as imperative with plastic) to prevent the sun scorching the leaves. Insert canes vertically into the compost, approximately 10 cm (4 in) from the planting hole, and tightly attach a cane horizontally at the top, middle and bottom (the bottom one being around 15 cm (6 in) from the compost surface). In the gaps between the horizontal canes run wire or strong string so that you have either a cane or wire/string running horizontally at 30 cm (12 in) intervals. This will allow you to support the side shoots and the fruit that grows. You can avoid the wire/string horizontals by using pea netting if you prefer. Melons do have tendrils and will attach themselves to the netting, but some will still require tying in.

As the plant grows, one main stem will develop: this is the leader. The leader should be trained to grow vertically by loosely tying it to the bamboo cane with twine. Melon stems are vulnerable to damage so should be tied in using a loose loop, with the knot being tied to the cane. This should allow the stem to move about and have room to expand without putting pressure on it. Should the leader reach the top of your support then the growing tip should be pinched out or cut off. This will then increase the amount of side shoots produced. Melon flowers, particularly females, are produced in the most abundance on the side shoots (laterals), and the shoots from these side shoots (sub-laterals), so the more you can encourage, the greater your chances of fruit are. Melons which are grown well and healthily will produce laterals and sub-laterals freely, but you can encourage them further by pinching out the lateral after five leaves have formed, and pinch out the sub-lateral at two or three leaves. Pinching only produces small wounds that heal quickly so the risk of infection is low. These laterals and sub-laterals should be loosely tied into the frame horizontally where practicable.

They can be successfully trained up strong string as per tomatoes and cucumbers. The string should be fixed firmly to the ground by the plant using a peg hammered into the ground. If you are growing in pots or grow bags, the end of the string should be tied around the pot/grow bag or be placed in the planting hole, and the melon planted onto the string with the developing roots holding it in place. The top of the string should be fixed to a strong structural support of the greenhouse or polytunnel as it needs to bear the weight of the plant and its fruit. Twist the leading stem around the string as it grows, and tie in the laterals to the string as they develop.

WATERING

As already discussed, both melons and watermelons require a moist but free-draining growing medium. In reality this means that the compost is not dry but nor is it waterlogged; when inspected the compost should have a darker colour (rather than light and dusty) but the compost should not yield water when pressed gently. It should not be allowed to dry out completely either. Where possible, use rainwater and bring it up to ambient temperature, or even better a little warmer. The easiest way to do this is to fill up a watering can or bottle and place it in the greenhouse or polytunnel, either the night before or in the morning, and let the sun warm it up. This is always preferrable to putting cold water on the roots, the area where melons desire the most warmth.

Never, under any circumstances, water from above or spray the leaves and stems with water, even for a short time. Melon leaves are very susceptible to fungal diseases that prefer damp conditions on foliage. Spraying with water is also a sure way to create stem rot, as the water runs down the plant leaves and stem, and eventually sits where the stem meets the compost. This, combined with the moist conditions subsequently created around the lower stem, can kill a small or mature plant equally quickly.

Regular gentle watering is the best solution to this. When the plant is growing at seedling stage and growing on until planted out, water regularly with small amounts of water. The best way to gauge this is to cover the surface with vermiculite (which will also help to prevent stem rot), as it changes colour and dries out when it requires watering. Water gently with a small watering can, or a bottle with a watering nozzle attached, and apply only around the edges of the pot, away from the stem. As soon as water comes out of the bottom stop watering and move it somewhere to drain. Never leave the pots standing in water.

During the period just after the plants have been planted into their final positions continue to water gently around the planting zone using the water bottle or small watering can method. Once the plants have put out roots and begun growing rapidly, usually by mid-June, it may be easier to change watering methods to make sure they stay moist. If you are growing in pots or grow bags, and are available to tend your plants once or twice a day during hot weather, it is possible, and a good option, to continue to water with the water bottle or small watering can method. Water when the surface of the compost starts to become dry, particularly during spells of hot weather. If there is a spell of dull, cooler or rainy weather, then don't be in rush to water, as the plants will slow down in growth and only sit in cold wet soil, which increases the chances of root rot. It is much better during less favourable conditions to not water at all than overwater. The effects of underwatering can be corrected, whereas overwatering can cause much more damage, often irreversible. Obviously, the plants do not want to go through periods of significant wilt as this can damage the cell structure, which it cannot recover from. Slight wilting is not usually an issue.

If the plants cannot be tended daily, then a drip watering system is an excellent option. It provides regular, gently applied water direct to the compost. Remember to turn off the drippers during colder dull spells to prevent the plant's roots sitting in water in suboptimal conditions.

Plants grown outside with a black plastic or weed-proof membrane mulch will require watering much less than those in pots, as the roots are not restricted and can go out looking for moisture. Watermelons in particular need more water than people tend to think, especially when the fruit is swelling. The general rule of thumb is to apply 2 to 5 cm (1 to 2 in) of water per week in sunny warm weather. If it is overcast, cool and the compost is moist, then skip watering until the weather warms up again. There are a few ways to apply the water they need. Firstly, by cutting holes into the membrane (ideally one hole at each side of the plant) and sinking a plastic pot 2 cm or so into the compost. Water is then applied from a watering can into these pots and allowed to soak in. Woven weed-proof membrane will also allow water to permeate through it, so it can be applied directly to the membrane, however, this is not very controlled and risks water getting onto the stems and leaves, leading to fungal problems. It is better to use the sunken pot watering method. If a soaker hose (sometimes called a leaky hose or leaky pipe) is to be used, gently supplying water over a longer period, then this should be run under the membrane prior to planting.

If the compost dries out significantly and the plants have wilted, the temptation is to give them lots of water all at once to correct the problem quickly. The urge to do this with melons should be avoided, as sudden flushes of water will split the stems (which they can recover from, but which creates a vulnerable point for potential infection), or even worse, the fruit. As the fruit is growing the skin is thin, and when it nears ripening and is at full size a surge of water can crack open the fruit, exposing the moist flesh which will quickly rot. The emotion of the gardener, when this happens, cannot be described in words. To prevent these issues, water should be administered very gently over a period of time – drip feeders and bottle top watering nozzles are good for this. Apply a small amount and let it soak in, then return to it shortly afterwards and do the same. Do this over the course of a day or a few hours until the compost is moist again, but do not rush it. The plant will recover, split fruit will not.

As the fruit begins its process of ripening, the watering should be reduced to maximise the amount of sugar in the flesh. In a good year with most varieties, this process will start in early August; the fruit will have remained the same size for a noticeable period, and then the leaves of the plant will start to deteriorate by wilting and turning brown. This can cause a panic among growers and a temptation to water because the leaves are wilting, but this should be avoided if the compost is moist and there is well developed fruit, as the plant will have started the ripening process and will not be wilting from lack of water. At this point the plant is no longer growing but concentrating all its energy on producing fruit and viable seeds, so it is not demanding water for growth, only to sustain the remaining leaves. Watering should be reduced to such a level that they do not wilt due to lack of water. The best way to do this is to keep the compost on the dry side and add small amounts of water if the remaining green leaves begin to wilt. With some melon varieties the leaves die back almost completely as the fruit ripens, at this point little or no water should be applied.

Feeding

Both melons and watermelons grow rapidly and produce heavy fruits, so it should be no surprise that they require feeding regularly to maintain this growth. When the young plants are being grown on in their small pots ready for planting out, they can be fed with a weak general liquid feed after the first two weeks. If they are to be grown in pots then a handful of all round granular fertiliser, such as fish, blood and bone, should be mixed in with the compost prior to planting. A similar fertiliser should be applied to the surface of the compost at the same stage when you are growing the melons directly in the ground.

Once the melons start to produce flowers they will benefit from a liquid high potassium feed, applied weekly until the fruits stop swelling, when the plant stops growing and starts the ripening process. As ever, the feed should be applied gently, without flushing the compost with water. If weather conditions are poor and the compost is moist, then put off feeding as you would watering, until the weather has picked up again: liquid feeding at this time will only mean the plants sit wet and cold.

Pollination

Melons and watermelons, like pumpkins and cucumbers, are monoecious plants: they produce both male and female flowers on separate structures on the same plant. The male flowers, which

Female melon flower

Male melon flower

always appear first and in larger numbers, carry the pollen, and can be recognised by a thin stalk and no swelling behind the flower. The female flowers have an embryo fruit noticeable at the base of the flower, and require the pollen to be transferred from the male flowers to their stigma, from where it fertilisers the immature fruit.

In nature the process of pollination is carried out by flying insects visiting each flower, taking the pollen with them and depositing it on the female flowers. Gardeners can help this process by ventilating indoor growing areas by opening doors and windows, particularly on warm sunny days. Insects will quickly find the flowers and begin their work. It is also helpful to keep the humidity down during pollination time.

The pollination process can also be helped along by hand pollinating the female flowers. To do this the male flowers need to be removed by pinching them off with the stalk attached. Next, carefully remove all the petals to expose the pollen-carrying part of the flower, and gently rub it on the stigma in the middle of the female flower. The pollen grains are very small and difficult to see on melons, but are much more noticeable on watermelons and the female parts easier to access. Some growers also remove the petals from the female flower to increase the surface area of the stigma to work with, however, this can

MELONS & OTHER CUCURBITS

risk damaging the embryo fruit at the base of the flower if not done carefully. The ideal time to pollinate is on a warm sunny day around mid-morning, when the flowers have recently opened, the pollen is active and the female flowers most receptive. If this window has been missed and flowers are open and available, then pollination should still be attempted. Aim for at least two males to be used to pollinate each female, but use more if they are in abundance.

If fruit has set, the embryo will quickly start to swell once the petals die back. If it has failed, the fruit will turn yellow and drop off. Patience is required in high quantities during pollination, as many more female flowers fail than take. In watermelons the success rate can be around 50%, and in melons as low as 10%. If true seed is not required, then a mixture of opening the growing environment to insects and hand pollination will provide the greatest chances of success.

Pollinating by hand

Thinning the Fruit

Removing fruit which has set is a difficult task, not because it requires a lot of skill, but because it feels awful. Having nurtured these plants, trained them, watched them flower, hand pollinated them and have the fruit set, you are now being told to remove some of the potentially delicious melons and compost them. It is awful. This process is called thinning, and by doing so it improves flavour, maximises size and ensures that all the set fruit ripen. If too many fruit set, it places too much demand on the plant and results in small melons. Plants grown in pots or grow bags should be limited to three (or potentially four for a smaller fruited variety such as '*Minnesota Midget*'), and up to four when grown in the open ground or hot bed. When the fruits are the size of a walnut the best and largest should be selected to grow on to full size. Only one fruit per side shoot should be allowed to stay, two per side shoot can result in inferior melons.

Watermelons grown in the open ground tend to become a mass of side shoots and leaves, which makes it difficult to determine which side shoot they have come from. If it can be identified, then minimise to one per side shoot, but do not worry overly, and limit to no more than four fruits per plant. If really large watermelons are desired, limit to two or even one fruit per plant. The best way to detach a fruitlet is to cut them rather than pinching them off, as this gives a clean cut which is less likely to be a point of infection. Watermelons grown in containers, including grow bags, should not be allowed to grow more than two fruits per plant.

Melon and watermelon vines tend to die back as the fruit is ripening, which creates a problem if there are fruits which have set a significant time after the others. As the early setting ones ripen and the plant starts to die back, the later fruits can run out of time to mature sufficiently to a stage where they can ripen. To avoid this, ideally all fruits should set within a ten-day window. This is not set in stone, and if another fruit is set after twelve days there is no rush to remove it because it is two days past the preferred window. Sometimes a plant can set a solitary fruit early (mid-June) and while this is exciting it should be removed if there are no other female flowers being produced or setting at this time. The plant will focus all its energy on this one fruit at the subsequent expense of producing any more viable female flowers or fruit. Wait a few days, and if the plant is continuing to produce more female flowers and another two or three set within the next week to ten days then leave the early fruit and the plant will most likely deliver an early crop of melons.

Supporting the Fruit

Once the embryo melons have set, they grow quickly, become heavy and require some form of support to prevent them becoming damaged or falling from the plant. If the fruit has set low down, close to the compost level, or the plants are being grown along the ground, then they will need to be raised off the compost; if they are allowed to sit on the damp compost there is a chance they will rot. Anything with a flat surface that does not absorb water (therefore wood should be avoided) such as a flat stone, a piece of slate, an old plate or upturned plant pot saucer can be used. Gently lift the fruit and place your chosen item under it, avoid resting it on the stem, or close to it, to prevent it becoming damaged, and lower the fruit. Check regularly as the fruit grows to make sure no part of the melon is touching the compost surface. Most watermelons are grown along the ground and should also be supported in the same way (even if they are sitting on plastic mulch or weed membrane), though they will require a larger object as they grow much bigger than melons and have a larger surface area touching the support.

For melons which are grown vertically the best way to support the fruit is by reusing the net bag from bought fruit, such as oranges and lemons, or making a cradle from tights. These take the pressure off the stems by holding the weight of the fruit, and also catch them if they ripen quickly and fall from the vine. The support should be put in place when the fruit is about the size of a golf ball. When using a net bag, thread some twine or string through either end and place the fruit into the net bag then tie the string to a strong support, such as a horizontal cane/wire or the structure of the polytunnel or greenhouse. It should be tied tight enough to support the weight of the fruit currently and be able to stretch as the fruit swells. Tights are also an excellent option as they are strong and stretch easily to support the developing melon. The lower part of each leg, including the toe part, should be cut off, and holes made on either side with string being threaded through each side. The melon should then be placed inside, sitting in the toe section, and the tight tied to supports, as with the net bag method. Squares of material cut from tights can also be used to make slings, with string being threaded through each corner. It is important not to have the string or net bag pressing against the stem on which the fruit has set, as this can cut into it or cause it to snap entirely.

Harvesting Melons

Judging the ripeness of a melon can sound like a complicated process but there are many signs to help you harvest at the correct time. As you grow a certain variety multiple times and your experience builds up you will know exactly when to pick your favourite types for maximum texture and flavour. In most instances melons ripen as the vine dies; the leaves start to wilt, turn yellow and brown, and the stem can also dry up. Do not be tempted to dig up and throw away plants where the vine

Supporting melons using nylon tights

Watermelon tendril

looks dead but the fruit is not fully ripe, because left in place, as long as there is still some warmth in the sun, the melons will ripen.

Melon growers often use the terms 'full-slip' and 'half-slip' to describe one of the main signs of ripening. When most melons are approaching ripeness small cracks begin to appear where the stem meets the fruit. The half-slip stage is where it would still require a degree of force to separate it from the plant. Most melons are harvested at full-slip, which is where the cracks are well developed and the stem will detach from the fruit with a gentle touch. This sign, combined with a slight but quick change in colour, usually to a yellow tone, coupled with a melon scent from where the stem joins the fruit, will tell you it is ripe.

The smooth skinned Charentais type fruits of the *Cantalupensis* group, such as '*Petis Gris des Rennes*', '*Ogen*', '*Alvaro*' and '*Cantalun*', do not always crack and slip from the stem, so this should not be used as the main sign for ripeness. The best indicators to look for are a change in colour, usually to a yellow tone, which can happen quickly, and a melon scent which is apparent from the blossom end rather than the stalk end. If the thumbs are pushed gently around the blossom end and the fruit gives a little, this, combined with the other indicators, confirms that it is ripe.

The ripeness of melons in the Inodorus group is more difficult to determine because they generally do not give off any scent. One of the main indicators is that the fruit colour will change from green to yellow for '*Giallo d'Inverno*', and a light creamy green for some of the modern bred varieties such as '*Honeydew*'. Wait until all the green has changed colour and the skin is smooth and waxy; if it is dusty and dull then wait. As with the Charentais melons a squeeze of the blossom end with the thumbs will help: if it gives and springs back, then it is ripe, if it is solid and does not move, it is not yet ripe.

None of the melons increase in sugar content once they are

separated from the vine but their flesh does soften. Apart from the Inodorus group they do not store well and should be consumed at room temperature a short time after harvesting. If they are to be kept for a short time they should be stored in the refrigerator.

HARVESTING WATERMELONS

Watermelons do not display any of the ripeness signs that *Cucumis melo* do, and they require regular observation as they are a bit trickier to get exactly right. The main indicator that most growers look for is the drying out of the tendril. The tendril is the slender growth from the stem which curls around objects to support the vine. The important one to keep an eye on is the one joined to the stem that attaches to the fruit. The tendril should have fully turned brown and dried out before harvesting takes place. At the same junction as the tendril there is often a very small leaf which is referred to as a 'leaf ear', this will also turn brown as the fruit ripens. Sometimes there is no tendril present where the fruit stem grows from the vine. If this is the case then use the leaf ear drying out as the gauge.

The area of the watermelon which sits on the ground (or support) has a different colour to the rest of the fruit, this is called the 'ground spot' or 'field spot'. The changing of the ground spot colour to a creamy buttery yellow is another key indicator that the fruit is ready for picking. Look for the tendril to start drying and then gently lift and turn the fruit to observe the colour of the ground spot; if it is pale green or white then it is not ripe. The whole skin should also be observed regularly; it should change from bright and shiny to dull. If it is still bright it is unlikely to be ripe. At this stage of ripening the watermelon should show ribs along the fruit, another sign that the fruit is ripe.

Some growers count forty days from fruit set to harvest and

consider this to be the best indicator. This relies on two things, that the exact date of the fruit showing signs it has set is observed and noted, and that the weather is relatively consistent for the next forty days.

The technique of knocking the watermelon with a knuckle and if it sounds hollow then it is ripe has long been dismissed by experienced growers as an inaccurate indicator, as different sized fruits can sound different, and what sounds hollow to one person may not to another.

Using all the indicators discussed above (apart from knocking it to see if it sounds hollow) is the best way to accurately determine the ripeness. Firstly, closely observe the tendril and when it is turning brown gently check the ground spot, if it has changed to a buttery yellow then harvest, if it hasn't, wait for the tendril to dry out fully and check the ground spot again. Do this while observing the change in skin colour from bright to dull, and the development of ribs. If all or most of these criteria are met the watermelon is ripe. Try to make notes of the variety and what these indicators were like at the time of harvest and whether it was slightly over or under ripe, so that harvesting can be adjusted in future.

Common Problems

Red Spider Mite

Primarily a problem of indoor growing areas. The small red spiders suck the plant sap and create a fine silky webbing over the leaves and stems. The foliage becomes discoloured, bleached and sometimes speckled. The growth on new leaves and shoots becomes stunted and can be severe enough to cause leaf loss and plant death. The best treatment is preventative, as once a bad infestation has got hold the mites are difficult to remove. Spider mites dislike a damp atmosphere so increase the humidity by damping down the greenhouse or polytunnel floor regularly (sometimes multiple times daily) during hot spells. Under no circumstances be tempted to spray or wet the leaves as this will create other, potentially more severe, problems.

Fusarium Wilt

This is a fungal disease which is found in soil. There are many different strains of this fungus which effect different groups of plants. When it enters the plant and gets into the water-carrying xylem vessels, the plants try to defend themselves by producing a gum which causes the vessels to become blocked. The first sign of this disease in melons and watermelons is a sudden wilting of the leaves due to the lack of water being able to flow to them. Wilting can also be a sign of root rot or simply due to the plant being in direct hot sun. If the soil is moist and the wilting does not recover overnight, then it could be fusarium wilt. A key diagnostic tool is to cut a leaf that is wilting from the plant with some of the leaf stalk attached. If a dark ring is present in the cross section of the leaf stalk then it is most likely fusarium wilt. The cut leaf stalk can also be pushed gently back to the cut surface on the plant and then drawn back away; if the sap is viscous and stretches across the gap as the leaf is pulled away that is also a sign of the disease. There are no treatments once it is discovered but it can be prevented by changing the soil each year or rotating away from where cucurbits have been grown in the last three or four years. If the fungus is known to be present in the soil, grow resistant watermelon varieties or grow in containers with bought in compost. Destroy any plants that have been infected with fusarium wilt.

Verticillium Wilt

Verticillium wilt is another soil-borne fungal disease which causes very similar symptoms to fusarium wilt; however, the leaves tend to turn yellow from the lower leaves upward. The biggest cause is the plant sitting in cold wet soil for prolonged periods, therefore if cool or overcast weather is forecast avoid watering until temperatures warm up again, which will also help to avoid root rot and stem rot. The fungus can remain in the ground, so replace the soil, grow in containers with fresh compost, or rotate the growing area.

Anthracnose

Another fungal disease which effects melons and watermelons, anthracnose can remain in the soil for a prolonged period while also being hosted on plant debris and passed down through seeds to the next generation of plants. Its spores are transferred to plants when favourable cold and damp conditions are present, particularly if water is allowed to sit on the leaves. Spots appear on the leaves and grow quickly with each spot having a yellow halo. The infected areas turn brown and dry, and cause the whole leaf to die. If identified, the leaves should be removed and destroyed, but if a bad infection takes place the whole plant may need to be destroyed. There is no treatment, but indoor growing areas should be well ventilated and water should be prevented from touching the leaves. Soil and compost should be replaced and rotation take place. Some varieties of watermelon and cucumber are resistant to anthracnose infection.

Mildew

Mildew is a form of fungus that can affect a wide group of plants, attacking foliage, stems and flowers by covering them with a white powdery coating. It causes a weakening of the plant, distorted growth and potential death. It can occur on both indoor and outdoor grown plants, and is problematic where the soil is dry but the atmosphere humid. It can often occur at the end of the growing season when the plants are in their ripening phase and night-time temperatures are becoming cooler. At this stage it is not of concern and will not affect the crop. Keeping the compost just moist during warm weather is the best preventative method. There are chemical treatments available for powdery mildew, but some growers report good success by spraying leaves with a 40/60 ratio mix of milk and water every ten days or so. This should be a last resort for melons and watermelons (but can be more freely tried with the other cucurbits) as wetting the leaves should be avoided at all costs.

Blossom End Rot

Blossom end rot, as its name implies, attacks the area of the young fruit where the blossom was, which begins to turn brown and black and rots away, leaving the fruit unable to reach maturity. The cause of this is lack of calcium in the plant. Irregular watering, particularly when the fruit has just set and is swelling quickly, causes a fluctuation in calcium being taken up by the roots. Aim to keep the compost moist, not wet, during the growing and fruiting phase. It is also important to use the correct liquid feed with a higher potassium concentration, such as a tomato feed, because a high nitrogen content fertiliser will encourage an increased formation of leaves, which in turn will create a high demand on calcium, diverting it away from the fruits.

Stem Split

This problem generally occurs low on the stem, often between the first true leaves and the compost level. There are two main causes of stem split. The first is a sudden change in temperature over a few days from cold to warm. This is especially an issue early on in the season when the temperatures are erratic and the plant is growing quickly. A sudden change from cold weather, when the plant will slow down or grow slowly, to hot weather will cause the plant to respond quickly. This sudden surge in growth can cause the fragile stem to split. The second cause of stem split is irregular watering, usually a drying out of the compost followed by a sudden flush of water. If the plant has wilted or the compost has dried out, then it must be watered very gently to re-moisten it, otherwise stem split (and fruit split at that stage) will invariably occur. Do not be tempted to flush through water in a panic that the plant is wilting. Gently provide a little water, let it soak in, return in an hour or so and do the same. More damage will be caused by overwatering than underwatering. Stem split is a significant point of weakness for infections but also for stem rot to take place, particularly if near to compost level. If it does occur, the wound should be kept dry and a good dusting of yellow sulphur will help prevent infection. Unless the split is severe, with the correct care most plants grow on without any problems and fruit as normal.

Overwatering

A sure sign of overwatering is the leaves starting to turn yellow. As the compost becomes saturated with water, oxygen is pushed out of the soil which prevents nutrients being absorbed, and if the roots sit in water for a prolonged period, particularly during a cold spell, they will quickly begin to rot. If the overwatering is caught quickly, the plant will recover, if not, the plant may continue to lose vigour and eventually die. Aim to make sure the compost is just moist, not wet, particularly during the quick growing phase, and that it doesn't sit in water. All pots, grow bags etc. should be raised from the surface they are placed on to allow excess water to drain away. If in doubt, stay on the drier side than wet.

Plants Producing Small Fruits

Some varieties of melon, such as '*Minnesota Midget*' and '*Golden Midget*' produce smaller than average fruits but if the fruit being produced is smaller than expected there are some potential reasons. Irregular watering while the fruit is swelling quickly after being set is a common cause, as is not feeding regularly, usually weekly, with a high potassium fertiliser once the melons begin to develop. Allowing too many fruits, such as more than three or four (depending on the variety and growing method), will invariably end in smaller and less satisfying melons. Some plants, as described in the Thinning the Fruit section above, set one fruit very early which dominates nutrients and prevents others setting or keeps them small. If this is the case, the first one should be removed early in its life.

Growing Timeline

Mid-April:
Sow seed using the wet paper towel method or direct into pots and keep heated.

May-June:
Once seeds have germinated and seedlings are beginning to grow their first true leaf, take off heat during warm days and place in sun without cover. Re-cover and heat overnight.

Late May-Early June:
Once overnight temperatures are reliably over 10°C and the days are warm (not rainy and overcast) plant into their final growing positions. In a good spring, and depending on where in the UK they are being grown, this can be late May or the first week in June. For North America, check your USDA hardiness zones for the most accurate dates.

Late June-July:
Keep plants moist but not overwatered. Female flowers should be opening from the last two weeks of June and throughout July. When they start to flower, feed weekly with high potassium liquid feed. Open indoor growing environments and hand pollinate to aid fruit set. Remove covers from outdoor plants when warm and sunny, only

cover through cool and rainy periods. Once the required number of fruits have set, remove all others which set.

August-September:
When the fruits stop swelling and the plants begin to enter their ripening phase (usually in the first two weeks of August in a good year for melons, though it can be later, and late August into September for watermelons), signified by the leaves starting to wilt, turning yellow and/or brown, then reduce watering. Watering should be only of a level to prevent the plants from wilting. The compost can be allowed to dry out on the surface between each watering. Only water lightly and gently, enough to re-moisten the surface. If in doubt under-water rather than overwater. Keep an eye on melons for signs of ripening, change in colour, scent and cracking where the stem meets the fruit. If unsure, double check the ripening signs for your variety. Check the watermelon's tendril for drying out and examine the ground spot for it changing to a buttery yellow colour. As soon as the ripeness signs are met, harvest and savour your sweet and juicy melons and watermelons fresh from the vine.

October to February:
Start planning the melons you are going to grow next year and order the seed.

SAVING SEED

Melons and watermelons are very promiscuous and will readily cross-pollinate with other varieties from the same genus. A watermelon (*Citrullus lanatus*) will only cross with another watermelon, and melons (*Cucumis melo*) with other melons. The resulting seeds of a crossed fruit will produce a range of offspring with varying quality and size, which is of no use unless you are plant breeding. Therefore, if you wish to save your own seed because you have a melon which has been difficult to obtain, then you need to isolate the flowers and ideally hand pollinate.

F1 seeds (also labelled as F1 Hybrid) are a first generation cross deliberately created by crossing two known parent varieties to produce offspring which has specific characteristics, such as early setting fruit, quick growth or cold tolerance. They are chosen by growers as they reliably produce excellent results. The seed produced by an F1 plant, even grown in isolation, will not produce the same fruit as its parent, therefore you cannot save seeds from it. It also means that the cross has to be made every year by the seed supplier, hence the higher cost of the seed.

Some varieties, such as '*Melba*' and '*Cal Sweet*', are not F1s or old enough to be classed as heritage, so they will reliably produce offspring true to the parent if they are grown in isolation or hand pollinated.

To successfully save true seed you need to prevent cross-pollination. There are different ways to do this but the two most simple are to grow in isolation or cover the flowers to prevent bees and other pollinators getting to the pollen. Isolation is the process of growing a variety you want to save seed from away from other varieties that may cross with it. It does mean that you will only be able to grow one variety that year. If you are growing on an allotment or close to other people who are growing melons there is a small risk that a bee could transfer pollen from another area and contaminate your seed, but from garden to garden this is unlikely. Therefore, it is possible to allow pollinators in your growing area to move from flower to flower and also carry out hand pollination, which should then produce true seed.

The other method when growing multiple varieties in the same space is to cover each flower and then hand pollinate each one. This is the method chosen by dedicated seed savers and it ensures the seed will be true. The easiest method is to source some small organza bags and select up to five male flowers per one female and before they have opened cover them gently with the organza bags. This will stop pollinators getting to the pollen. As soon as the flowers have opened follow the hand pollination method described earlier and as soon as you have completed the process recover them with the bags, again preventing something visiting the flower after you have done your work. As soon as the flower dies back and the fruit begins to swell the bag can be removed. It is good practice to then mark this fruit with a loop of bright cotton or a cable tie. This should always be a very loose, wide loop and never tight to the stem, as it could cut into the stem when it swells.

It is important that the melon is fully ripe in order for the seeds to be viable. The seed in a melon is all contained in the central cavity so it is easy to scoop out, whereas in a watermelon the seeds are distributed throughout the flesh, so they require a little bit more effort to remove. Wash the removed seeds in a colander under cold water to remove the flesh and the bulk of the gelatinous coating. They can be soaked in a cup of water for a few hours to remove any gel left on if you want to be thorough. Turn out the seeds onto some kitchen towel or cardboard and dry at room temperature, turning the seeds regularly and making sure they do not stick to the paper. Once dry, put the seeds in an airtight container or bag and store somewhere cool and dark. Stored in the correct conditions they can remain viable for up to five years, but ideally you should grow them again before then and share any spares with friends.

Heritage Seeds

In the UK we use the term 'heritage' to refer to seed which is old and/ or has historic importance. In North America they use 'heirloom' instead of 'heritage', and the two terms are often interchangeable in the UK. There is debate over what constitutes the designation 'heritage', some say that it is any variety over fifty years old, while others believe it to refer to pre-Second World War varieties, or prior to the mechanisation of agriculture. What generally strikes a chord for heritage enthusiasts is the historical story attached to the variety and the responsibility of keeping it alive. Once a variety is lost it is extinct, a fate which has sadly befallen many vegetables and all but two of the many melons bred in the walled gardens of Victorian England. Keeping varieties alive is important because they offer genetic diversity, which could be useful for breeding new plants in a changing world and climate. Fortunately, the Heritage Seed Library, part of Garden Organic, maintains a range of heritage fruit and vegetable seeds, and distributes them to members. There is an array of heritage melon and watermelon varieties available to buy and these have been highlighted in the varieties list section.

Recommended Varieties of Melon and Watermelon

Melons and watermelons have different maturing times between sowing and fruiting, depending on variety, which is measured in days. You may see this information in the variety description on the seed packet or on the internet. These figures are obviously under ideal conditions, but they do give you a good indication of your chances of producing a delicious melon before the season runs out. Early varieties are ready in 80 days or less, midseason varieties between 80-90 days, and late varieties take 90 days or more. In the UK, varieties listed at more than 90 days should be avoided unless you have heating or have developed a reliable method and there is a variety you really want to try. Varieties that take over 100 days to mature are sadly not a realistic option.

The further north you live in the UK, the shorter the number of days to fruit you want to grow, with Scotland and the far north of England concentrating on the earlies. In general, Yorkshire and the Midlands region can, with protection, push to the midseason types, and in the south, well, you can take your pick of the 90 days or less varieties. These, of course, are recommendations, and beginners should start with the early and the F1 varieties. Once you have built up confidence and a growing method that works for you, then you should challenge this. On a positive note, there are a great variety of melons and watermelons to try that fall into the early and midseason categories.

In North America it is useful to refer to the hardiness zones of each area as a guide to the days to frost, and match this up to the listed days to fruiting.

Russia, Ukraine and a lot of the Eastern European and former Baltic states have developed a large range of reliable short season and cold tolerant melons and watermelons which are worth searching the internet for if you want to try something really different. The varieties have not been listed here as they are not always readily available.

Melon (*Cucumis melo*)

'*Ananas*' (Heritage)
Generally late in the UK climate but the plant tends to hold on longer than others so is reliable. Can be a vigorous and scrambling grower which needs frequent tying in to keep it organised. Very sweet and firm honey cream flesh is contained in a fruit covered completely in a fine netting. Best to limit to two or three fruits per plant to get reasonable sized fruit with maximum flavour.

'*Alvaro*' (F1) (RHS Award of Garden Merit)
A smooth Charentais type melon with orange skin and grey/green

Four leaf stage of the *Cantalun* melon

stripes housing a rich, aromatic and sweet salmon-coloured flesh. Good results from outside growing in RHS trials.

'Blenheim Orange' (Heritage)
Bred by William Crump, head gardener at Blenheim Palace, and winner of an award at the RHS show of 1880. One of the two British bred heritage varieties that still exist. Readily available from seed suppliers. If you are interested in preserving history, you should buy seed and grow to help keep the variety on the market. Under cover it is a reliable netted green melon with orange flesh that has a wonderful flavour. Worth growing for this alone.

'Cantalun' (Heritage)
Currently only available from the Heritage Seed Library. An early to midseason Charentais type melon which can be prolific at producing fruits 12 to 15 cm (5 to 6 in) in diameter with a sweet firm orange flesh, and with a strong melon scent. Thin to three or four fruits per plant for maximum size and flavour.

'Charentais' syn. *'Cantaloupe di Charentais'* (Heritage)
The classic true Charentais melon famous in Provence. Small fruits have a light grey-green smooth skin with darker green ribs, and contain bright orange flesh with excellent flavour. Ideally to be grown under cover for maximum success. Look for the change in colour of the skin, and scent from the blossom end of the fruit, as signs of ripeness rather than waiting for cracking to appear at the stem, which may not occur.

'Collective Farm Woman' syn. *'Collective Farmer's Wife'* (Heritage)
The best type of Inodorus melons to try if these are your favourite types to eat. Starts off green and turns orange when ripe, with a very sweet pale flesh. Earlier producing and more cold tolerant

than '*Giallo d'Inverno*'. Seed not always readily available but worth searching out and then saving your own seed.

'*Early Frame Prescott*' syn. '*Prescott Hatif*' (Heritage)
An old French melon which looks more like a pumpkin. Heavily ribbed, sometimes with warts, the green/grey skin quickly turns a straw yellow and slips from the vine when ripe. Produces a more subtle scent than others and has a gentle, but sweet, melon flavour. Traditionally forced into fruit early at large estates on hot beds, which makes it a reliable cropper in shorter season areas under normal cultivation. The melon of choice for Monet's 1872 painting *Still Life with Fruit*.

'*Eden's Gem*' syn. '*Rocky Ford*' (Heritage)
Introduced onto the American market in the early 1900s. A small and heavily netted green skinned melon with green flesh which is tinged salmon around the seed cavity. Plants can be vigorous and prolific, so thin fruits judiciously. Excellent melon flavour. Some growers recommend harvesting at half-slip, when the cracks start to appear where the stem meets the fruit but before it detaches fully. Can be difficult to find seeds but '*Green Nutmeg*' is a more than adequate replacement while you are searching for them.

'*Emir*' (F1) (RHS Award of Garden Merit)
Cold tolerant and fast growing, producing sweet melons with a soft and very juicy orange flesh. Its green grey skin turns slightly orange and gives off a strong fragrance when ripe. Cracks around the stem and slips from the vine when in prime condition for eating. Good choice for beginners and growing outdoors with protection.

'*Giallo d'Inverno*' (Heritage)
Casaba type melon from Italy. A late variety which requires hot

conditions, so best grown under cover. Not the easiest to grow but if these are your favourite type of melon this is a good choice to try, as it has the traditional canary yellow skin with very sweet creamy flesh.

'Green Nutmeg' (Heritage)
An early to midseason heavily netted musk melon, first noted around 1830. The small fruits contain a light green flesh and were prized in America for their wonderful aroma and rich sweet taste. Fruits ripen to a yellowish-brown colour. Aim for three to four melons per plant and try to harvest just before the fruit separates from the vine. A rambling plant which can be a challenge to train, but do not let that put you off. A good choice for beginners interested in heritage varieties, and for growing in polytunnels or trying outside with protection.

'Hales Best Jumbo' (Heritage)
Bred by a Japanese farmer in California and introduced in 1925, this is a relatively small ribbed and heavily netted melon. It remains popular due to its earliness and the excellent flavour of its bright orange flesh, which some describe as an old-fashioned melon taste. A reliable variety to grow.

'Hero of Lockinge' (Heritage)
Introduced to the public by Sutton's Seeds in 1881, this is the second of the only two remaining British bred heritage melons that hasn't become extinct. Best bred under heated glasshouse cultivation so it can struggle to produce and set female fruits if conditions are not ideal. Late fruiting (usually September) and temperamental, but it is worth all the effort for its history and its small netted yellow fruit, which contain the most delicious white flesh. Once you have developed a trusted growing technique, or you can supply bottom heat, then make it your quest to find seed, grow it, enjoy it, and save the seed to help keep *'Hero of Lockinge'* alive.

'Honey Bun' (F1)

Compact plants suitable for containers and cold frame growing. Three to four fruits per plant. A good-looking heavily netted melon with sweet orange flesh. Good choice for beginners.

'Honeydew'

Very sweet variety with light green skin and flesh requiring long hot growing conditions. Harvest when the skin colour changes and the small leaf next to the fruit yellows. Needs to be cut from the vine as it will not crack around the stem. Arguably the best and most reliable variety of the Inodorus melons to try and grow.

'Jenny Lind' (Heritage)

A small heavily netted melon with a unique turban shape. Introduced in America in the 1840s and named after the famous singer Jenny Lind, who toured throughout the States in the mid-1800s. It was thought to be completely lost until some seeds were found in New Jersey and subsequently preserved and reintroduced by the American Seed Savers Exchange. Has quite a large cavity, but the firm green, sweet and spicy flesh is worth it. Early, cold tolerant and prolific. Fruit may need to be thinned.

'Malaga' (F1)

Recommended as a good replacement for the previously popular F1 melon *'Sweetheart'*. A thick ribbed, sweet, orange-fleshed melon. A reliable producer and it can be early.

'Melba'

Vigorous plants which claim to produce a generous crop of succulent, sweet, orange-fleshed oblong melons. A readily available variety which can be tried outdoors with protection.

'*Minnesota Midget*' (Heritage)
A very early, cold tolerant melon, bred at the University of Minnesota. Do not let the small cricket ball sized fruits deter you, this is an excellent sweet orange-fleshed melon. The fruits, which are prolific and can produce two crops, turn orange/yellow when ripe. An excellent heritage variety for beginners to try.

'*Noir des Carmes*' syn. '*Black Rock*' (Heritage)
One of the oldest French melons which has been grown since at least the 1800s, if not before. Bred by Carmelite Monks and grown in the monasteries around the Tours region, it was offered by Carter's seed catalogue in the UK as far back as 1845. It has a unique dark green, almost black, heavily ribbed skin which quickly turns orange when ripe. It can crack quickly and heavily when ready to eat, so harvest it when the cracks appear but before they get so deep that it dries the flesh. A reliable variety well adapted for cooler short season areas. An excellent heritage variety for beginners to try.

'*Ogen*' syn. '*Ha'Ogen*' (Heritage) (RHS Award of Garden Merit)
A reliable small, early and very aromatic old variety, commonly thought to originate in Israel. A Charentais type melon which is noted for its excellent texture and flavourful green flesh. A reliable cropper and a good choice for beginners, but it should not be overlooked by experienced growers.

'*Outdoor Wonder*' (F1)
This has been bred to be cold tolerant and boldly claims to provide guaranteed harvests in the UK, even outdoors. A Galia type melon with pale green flesh. You should aim to produce three fruits per plant. Good resistance to mildew.

'Pepito' (F1)

An early and very reliable variety which can produce in the north of Scotland with protection. Rugby ball shaped fruits with fine netting and green ribs. It has a sweet, deep orange flesh which holds on well if ripeness indicators are missed or you are away for a few days. Resistant to fusarium wilt and mildew.

'Petit Gris de Rennes' (Heritage)

A very old small Charentais type melon from France. Originally grown by the Bishop of Rennes over 400 years ago and well adapted to cool climates. The flesh is bright orange and of excellent quality, some argue the best flavour of all the Charentais melons. The fruits have a grey-green skin which changes to mustard yellow when ripe, though do not wait until full colour change, harvest when the colour change is evident and the scent is emanating from the blossom end. The fruits can be vulnerable to damage so make sure they are prevented from sitting on the compost or mulch surface.

'Rampicante Zuccherino' (Heritage)

An Italian heritage variety the name of which translates as 'Climbing Sugar'. The classic melon for serving with prosciutto ham. A vigorous, early and productive melon with yellow/green skin and orange flesh.

'Sucrine de Tours' (Heritage)

A very old French melon dating to at least 1763. This heavily netted fruit has a strongly perfumed thick orange flesh and was a regular in Vilmorin-Andrieux seed catalogues. It is generally one of the later melons to ripen in the UK season.

'Zatta' (Heritage)

An old Italian melon often called 'Brutta ma Buono' meaning ugly but good. Looks more like a pumpkin than a melon due to its heavily ribbed and warted fruit, which turns orange as it ripens, and which contains wonderful, sweet orange flesh. Grown by Thomas Jefferson at Monticello, and also cultivated in Canada. A variety that is often reliable and will attract interest from fellow gardeners for its looks alone.

WATERMELON (*CITRULLUS LANATUS*)

'*Asahi Miyako*' (F1)

A cold tolerant and early, sometimes very early, good size watermelon from Japan. Sweet dark red flesh is contained inside green skin which sports almost black stripes. Vigorous and resistant to fusarium wilt and anthracnose.

'*Blacktail Mountain*'

Frequently voted the number one recommended watermelon for short season and colder climate areas by experienced growers due to its reliability, flavour and generous harvest window. This means growers do not have to be expert at observing ripeness signs to the same degree as other varieties. Originally bred by Glenn Drowns as a teenager, after being frustrated at not being able to grow watermelons in the short season of his home in the foothills of Blacktail Mountain, Idaho. One of the earliest and cold tolerant watermelon varieties, you will not be disappointed.

'*Cal Sweet*'

A modern bred 'bush' watermelon that has received an All-American Selection award (similar to the RHS Award of Garden Merit). Compact plants produce a traditional green striped, sweet red-fleshed fruit. A good choice for container growing, but aim for one fruit per plant if you do.

'Champagne' (F1)
Green rind icebox watermelon with fine, crisp, sweet yellow flesh.
Globe shaped fruit can weigh between 2 to 3.5 kg when ripe. Can
be tried in containers though this may restrict the fruit size.

'Charleston Grey' (Heritage)
Bred in 1954 in Charleston, South Carolina. It has a long-standing
reputation as a quality watermelon and is well known throughout
the Southern States of America. It is also grown commercially
around the world, including in Egypt, where the watermelon is
believed to have first been cultivated. An oblong fruit with light
green/grey skin which protects the delicious red flesh inside.
Very adaptable to different growing conditions and resistant to
fusarium wilt and anthracnose. Often the choice to make pickled
watermelon rind.

'Crimson Sweet' (Heritage)
With the right protection this is a good choice for northern climate
growers looking for the quintessential American watermelon. Can
produce large fruits if thinned to one or two per plant. Green
rind with dark green stripes and a bright crimson sweet flesh of
good flavour. Resistant to fusarium wilt and anthracnose. Seeds
are widely available.

'Cream of Saskatchewan' (Heritage)
A rare cream-fleshed watermelon brought to Saskatchewan,
Canada, by Russian immigrants. Light green skin with dark stripes
contains a sweet cream-coloured flesh that has excellent flavour.
Be aware of the brittle rind which, when ripe, has the habit of
bursting open if not handed gently. A good and interesting choice
for short season climates.

'Early Moonbeam'
An early icebox melon bred in Oregon, so a good choice for shorter season cold climate areas. A thin light green skin protects a crisp sweet and bright yellow flesh. A good choice for beginners looking for something reliable but different to impress their friends.

'Golden Midget' (Heritage)
Originally bred by Elwyn Meader and Albert Yeager at the University of New Hampshire in 1959. A very early and cold tolerant small fruited, red-fleshed variety which can be ready in as little as 70 days from germination. On most occasions it starts off green skinned and turns fully yellow when ripe, however it can show yellow skin earlier in the growing season. If this happens then use all other ripeness indicators before harvesting. Not quite as sweet as other watermelons but very juicy crisp flesh and an excellent variety to try for beginners, and suitable to grow in containers.

'Janosik' (Heritage)
A heritage variety from Poland named after Juraj Janosik, a legendary Slovakian outlaw similar to Robin Hood. Dark green rind and bright yellow sweet flesh which has excellent texture, never mealy. Early, cold tolerant and produces large fruits in shorter climates. One of the best yellow-fleshed watermelons.

'Klondike Blue Ribbon' (Heritage)
A large red-fleshed crisp watermelon that is listed at 80-90 days to fruit, which is pushing the edge of the UK growing season in a less favourable year. Grow under cover if possible. It is advisable to limit fruit to one or two per plant to maximise chances of success. Resistant to fusarium wilt. One to try once you have gained confidence.

'*Little Darling*' (F1)

A modern compact plant that grows up to 1.5 m and produces small elongated very dark green fruit with a very sweet red flesh. With protected growing you can aim to produce three to four fruits per plant. A good choice for container growing but plan on one or two fruits per plant.

'*Mini Love*' (F1)

Specifically bred for short season and cooler climates. A compact plant which produces high yields of single serving sweet deep red-fleshed watermelons. Can produce up to six fruits per plant in open ground, but reduce this number if being cultivated in pots. An All-American selection winner in 2017. Good resistance to anthracnose.

'*Moon and Stars*' (Heritage)

The quintessential and most famous heritage American watermelon. Revered by watermelon enthusiasts due to its unique green rind which is dotted with yellow 'stars' and often one large yellow spot, the 'moon'. A popular commercial variety in America in the early 1900s, it fell out of favour and was thought to be extinct until 1981 when it was found growing on a farm in Missouri and was subsequently reintroduced by the Seed Savers Exchange. It has a very sweet pink-red flesh, though a harder to find yellow-fleshed variety has also been introduced. Pushing the very end of the northern, short season growing climate, but if a reliable technique has been mastered and/or heating can be provided, then an attempt should be made at producing the heritage watermelon grower's dream.

'*Orangeglo*'

Not quite old enough to be classed as a heritage variety but has a strong following among enthusiasts due to its reliability. Large oblong fruits contain an amazing bright orange flesh with an excellent flavour, which some growers describe as the best flavoured watermelon there is. Good resistance to disease.

'Petite Yellow' (Heritage)
A small plant producing small watermelons with a light green rind with dark stripes. One of the earliest watermelons available with a sweet and aromatic yellow flesh. Good choice for growing in pots or in limited space.

'Sugar Baby' (Heritage)
An early small icebox watermelon with a very dark green, almost black, skin and red flesh, which in some years is not the sweetest but still with good flavour. Early, reliable and a great variety to choose for the beginner. Seeds readily available.

'Sweet Siberian' (Heritage)
An extremely old and short season cold tolerant watermelon from Russia that was introduced to the US in 1898. It fell out of commercial seed favour but was saved and maintained by the US Seed Savers Exchange before being reintroduced. The green rinded fruits can get to the size of a football and contain very sweet apricot-coloured flesh. Seeds can be difficult to obtain but it is worth the effort to search for them.

Pumpkins and squash

PUMPKINS, SQUASH AND COURGETTES IN THE GARDEN

BOTANICAL INFORMATION

All pumpkins are squash, but not all squash are pumpkins. Clear? Probably not. What we in the UK (and the US) call pumpkins are actually a type of winter squash, a type that develops a hard skin in the late autumn sun which allows them to be stored over the winter and into spring. However, not all winter squash are pumpkins. The traditional orange ribbed and smooth skinned winter squash that are associated with Hallowe'en are what we commonly call pumpkins. They can be either *Cucurbita pepo*, *Cucurbita maxima* or *Cucurbita moschata*. Summer squashes, which include courgettes (zucchini), marrows and patty pans, are eaten young and fresh while they are tender, and they do not store over the winter.

Therefore, let's refer to all this family as squash. Native and domesticated in Central America before making its way to the US, there are many identifiable types of squash, and while botanists argue over whether there are thirteen or thirty species (or somewhere in between), what gardeners generally need to concern themselves with are the main three: *Curcubita pepo*, *C. maxima*, and *C. moschata*. The other two domesticated species are *Cucurbita argyrosperma* and *C. ficifolia*, with the latter commonly referred to as '*Fig Leaved Gourd*' or '*Fig Leaf Gourd*'. *C. ficifolia* is notable for containing the '*Shark Fin Melon*', the pulp of which is used in Asian cooking to replace the expensive and often unobtainable shark fin in traditional shark fin soup.

Nutritional Benefits

Due to the wide range of colours, sizes and species, squashes contain different proportions of vitamins and minerals, but across the range they all provide high levels of fibre, which helps digestion, beta-carotene, high levels of vitamin A and C, as well as vitamin B6, a deficiency in which has been linked to depression. They also contain various antioxidants that have been linked to cancer prevention.

Growing Techniques

Squashes are much more forgiving to the grower than melons and watermelons but that does not mean their requirements should be taken lightly. To produce healthy plants, a good crop, and the most abundant and heaviest fruits they do need specific care and attention.

Requirements

Of all the cucurbit family, squashes – particularly pumpkins and other winter squash – are the fastest growing, largest plants, requiring the richest soil, the most watering and regular feeding. They can grow vast distances in multiple directions and can produce fruits weighing over 1000 kg. Courgettes and summer squash are more compact plants, but still require a lot of space, nutrients and water. Some varieties can be grown in large pots but most are not suitable.

They are the hardiest and therefore most suitable for outdoor cultivation without added protection, but do require full sun and well-drained, moisture retentive soil, with a pH between 6.0 and 7.0 to achieve the best results. Any period in shade will reduce the vigour of the plants. Excellent results will be achieved if cultivated under cover but they take up a large area in environments where space is at a premium. *C. moschata*, being native to Central and Southern America, requires the hottest and most protected sites available.

PROPAGATION

Squash seeds are generally larger than melon seeds and should be sown from mid-April to the first week of May, with one or two seeds to a 6 to 7 cm pot. Use a good quality compost and place the seeds on their side, as their flat surface can be susceptible to moisture sitting on the surface and rotting the seed before it can germinate. Cover with 1 to 2 cm of compost and finish with a layer of vermiculite or perlite if possible, though they will germinate fine without it. Place the pots in a propagator, or covered in a consistently warm place, and keep just moist while they germinate. Bottom heat will speed up the germination process, but remain patient with the *C. moschata* varieties which prefer more heat and can take longer to germinate. For rare seeds use the paper towel germination method discussed in the Propagation section for melons and watermelons.

If both seeds germinate then the weaker one can be snipped off at compost level, but if both seedlings are required they can be split and potted on individually, unlike melons and watermelons. When they have each produced one true leaf they can be gently tipped out of the pot and teased apart to separate, and then re-potted back into a 6 to 7cm pot to grow on. Whereas potting on is strongly advised against for melons and watermelons, due to root shock, squashes are more resilient (though not resistant) so potting on is necessary to achieve good sized specimens ready for planting out in early summer. Aim to pot on into a 10 to 14 cm pot, any bigger will make the plant difficult to handle when being transplanted into its final position. Grow on in a frost-free environment, and place them outside on sunny warm days to harden off, i.e. acclimatise to cooler conditions outside.

Planting out Squashes

Do not be tempted to plant out squashes too early as they will not thank you for it. They will simply sit in cold wet soil, which at the very least will hold their growth back and at the worst rot the roots and/or stem. They should not be planted before the risk of frost has passed, usually the last week of May in the south of the UK, and first week of June in the north, but they will benefit from another week or so in their pots if the weather is cooler than average.

Before planting, dig into the soil a generous helping of compost, well-rotted manure or other organic matter to the area where the squash are to be planted. Ideally this should be added over the winter or early spring, and allowed to work its way into the soil, but it can be dug in up to two weeks before planting, if necessary. As squashes grow vigorously and produce many large fruits in a short space of time, they require high levels of nutrition and moisture. If in doubt, add more organic material rather than being cautious with it.

Similar to when planting out melons, make a mound and gently place the plant in the top of it, to the same level as the compost in the pot. However, for squashes, it is good practice to make a shallow moat all around the base of the mound, this ensures that any water is transported away from the stem and directly to the root zone where it is needed to support the rapidly growing plant. Apply a generous handful of slow-release organic fertiliser, such as chicken manure pellets or fish, blood and bone to the surface of the compost.

Ideally, where possible, cover with a cloche or a garden fleece for the first two weeks. Make sure the plant is kept moist but not sitting in water for the first few weeks until it starts to grow rapidly, at which point the watering can be increased. One of the biggest causes of failure in squashes is applying too much water early in the season.

GROWING VERTICALLY

One of the biggest challenges for a lot of people growing squashes is that they do not have the room to accommodate a vine growing up to three metres in multiple directions. The solution to this is to train them up vertical supports. Bamboo canes will simply not cut the mustard here, something much stronger and rigid is required, such as hazel poles or a frame made from fence posts with a metal wire grid attached. The frame should ideally be two metres tall. Remember to check whether the squash is vining, rather than a bush variety, most summer squashes and courgettes do not grow long vines and therefore cannot be trained in this manner. This method also allows multiple plants to grow in the space one plant would take up if allowed to scramble across the ground. Plant the squashes at the base of the frame, spacing roughly one metre apart, using the same mound and moat method described earlier. The vines will need to be regularly tied and weaved through the frame to keep them under control. Any long branching vines making an attempt to escape can be pruned back to a leaf.

GROWING ON COMPOST HEAPS AND HOT BEDS

Squashes will grow very happily when planted on top of a compost heap or in a hot bed. The heat, high levels of nutrition and moisture will create huge growth both in the vine and fruit, so these areas are best saved for the larger varieties, rather than wasted on courgettes or summer squash, which are always prolific in regular garden beds. A mature compost heap will have some well decomposed material that has turned to compost for the squash to root into. Freshly filled heaps are not suitable for planting into. Remove any weeds from the top of the heap, and if there is some partially broken-down material on the top, cover with a good layer of fresh compost and then plant into it. Aim for one large squash plant per compost heap. The vine will soon have covered the heap and be at ground level and flowering.

Hot beds are best saved for the smaller, rarer *C. moschata* squashes, which require more heat than *C. pepo* and *C. maxima*. Build the hot bed (as described in the Growing in a Cold Frame or Hot Bed section for melons and watermelons) and plant one plant at two metre intervals using the mound and moat technique. The surface of the hot bed can be covered with black plastic to retain the heat produced and absorb more from the sun, which *C. moschata* will reward you with in fruit.

WATERING

The most common failures in squash growing are due to watering the incorrect amount and at the incorrect time, most notably too much too early, and not enough later in the season. Once planted, squashes, like other cucurbits, can appear to sit still, putting on little top growth, but after a short time the roots become established and the plant will soon be growing quicker than you can believe. The trick is not to water too much at this 'fixing' stage; make sure the compost does not dry out but only apply a small amount to gently moisten it if it does. Overwatering at this early stage, when cool nights and sub-optimal temperatures are the norm, will only cause the plants to sit in water and quickly rot away. Once the plant is growing rapidly, and after the fruit has set, it will require frequent watering and good doses of it, particularly during hot weather. Aim to keep the water well away from the stem and any fruit to prevent rot.

The leaves of squashes are large and frequently wilt in hot summer sun. This is caused by them losing moisture through transpiration quicker than the roots can replenish it. It is not usually a problem if the compost is moist and the plants recover at night when the temperature cools, then all is well. If they do not, they are too dry. If the temperatures are good, it is best to water in the evening; if not then do not rush into watering, water the next morning instead. In the heat and sun of midday, water will often evaporate quicker than it can be absorbed by the roots. If the soil is moist and the leaves do not recover and the problem gets worse, then it could be caused by fusarium wilt, but it is rare for this to affect squashes. Try to avoid overhead watering and sprinklers where possible, as frequently wet leaves can lead to mildew problems.

FEEDING

As squash plants grow quickly and produce many large fruit they require regular feeding to keep them growing at an optimum rate. On planting, apply a generous handful of organic slow-release fertiliser, such as fish, blood and bone, or chicken manure pellets, to provide nutrients throughout the season. The manure and compost added in advance of planting will get them growing nicely until they begin flowering, at which point a weekly dose of liquid high potassium feed, such as tomato fertiliser or liquid seaweed, will support further flowering and good fruit development. Once the fruits have reached their full size and begin changing colour, or the plants start to die back, the feeding can be stopped.

Thinning and Supporting the Fruit

Summer squashes and courgettes do not require thinning other than regular picking of the fruit and eating it. A good rule for this type of squash is that from the point at which the flower falls off they can be eaten, however, immature courgettes are delicious fried with the flower intact (before it has opened), and do not forget that the flower is excellent (whether stuffed or not) when dipped in batter and lightly fried.

Pumpkins and other winter squash can attempt to produce a large amount of fruit on the vine, and this can result in smaller than desired squash. In general, keep to no more than four fruits per plant. If larger ones are required then thin even more, even back to one fruit per plant.

Most winter squashes grow on trailing vines and the fruit ends up sitting on the ground. This is not usually an issue with summer squash and courgettes, as they have a bush habit and the fruit are produced close to the centre of the plant. They are also eaten quickly before they have time to sit on the compost too long. To prevent winter squashes from rotting or being damaged by slugs while they are sitting on compost for long periods it is good practice to raise them off the ground slightly. This can easily be done on flat pieces of stone or slate, or even pieces of wood. Bricks are not ideal because the fruit often outgrows them and falls back onto the ground. Purpose-built square racks can be made out of wood and slipped under the developing fruit and left in place until harvest.

Growing Large Pumpkins

The exact details of growing showstopping, record-beating large pumpkins are closely guarded secrets by expert growers, but there are a few things that can be done to supersize your fruits. For maximum size select either '*Atlantic Giant*' or '*Hundredweight*' varieties, any others will not be able to get in touching distance of those two. Growing them undercover will help significantly as they will be warmer, start growing more quickly and be protected from fluctuations in temperature. As indoor growing space is premium garden real estate, to dedicate a significant amount of it to growing potentially one pumpkin requires serious commitment, but it will be worth it.

Prepare the soil well, ideally with a good proportion of well-rotted horse manure over the winter or early spring before planting. Some growers add beer, milk and other secret nutrient cocktails to the can at every watering to boost growth. Good alternatives, until your own secret recipe has been developed, are comfrey feed or a diluted manure solution. To make life easier, fill a porous bag with comfrey leaves or manure and suspend it in a water butt. It will slowly create a weak fertiliser tea which can be applied at every watering. There are also some ready-made maxi-grow and giant veg fertilisers on the market which one can buy.

Unlike melons and watermelons, which also have long branching vines, squashes will produce roots from a node (a point on the stem where the growth of leaves and side shoots takes place) where it touches the compost. This helps boost plant growth by accessing more nutrients and moisture over a wide area, leading to larger fruits. This can be encouraged by choosing one node from different branches of the same plant and mounding compost up and around the node. Do not be tempted to overwater this mound but keep it lightly moist, only watering when it dries out, and the plant will quickly root into it.

As soon as the vine has set three or four fruits, thin to two, then once they are both starting to grow, thin down to one by removing the smallest of the two. Judicially remove new flowers as soon as you see them. Thinning to one fruit and removing subsequent flowers will allow all the energy to be diverted to the one superfruit.

Harvesting and Curing for Winter Use

Whereas summer squashes and courgettes should be used fresh, winter squashes can be harvested and stored to use over the winter and into the next spring. When it comes it harvesting, it is important not to harvest just because the fruits are at full size but rather when they are ripe. This way, they will store successfully for future use. Generally, the first signs are that the leaves begin to turn yellow, however some of the smaller varieties, such as '*Uchiki Kuri*', can be ready to use while others on the same plant are still growing. For maximum storage quality they should be left until the leaf colour change occurs and the skin turns a deep colour. The skin will also harden up significantly and if it resists the pressure of a fingernail then it is ready. Any leaves preventing the sun getting to the fruit can be removed later in the season to help speed up this process. Always cut the squash with secateurs, never tear them from the stem as this can create a wound for bacteria to invade and potentially cause rot back into the fruit. Make clean cuts in the stem above the fruit, ideally leaving a 'T' shape, containing two short sections of stem and the umbilical, the part which joins the fruit to the stem. As the 'T' stem dries it prevents bacteria getting into the fruit during storage.

Once removed from the plant, winter squash require a period of curing, which allows the skin to harden further, improving its storage qualities, and the heat from the sun helps to improve its flavour. Some growers leave the fruit in situ for this process to occur

MELONS & OTHER CUCURBITS

and remove it when the vine has completely died, but this relies on the weather being favourable at the beginning of autumn. A much more controlled way is to remove the fruits from the plant and place them on shelves or tables inside a greenhouse or polytunnel for a couple of weeks or so. This process can also be carried out on a sunny windowsill, but wherever it takes place the fruit should be turned every couple of days to ensure the sun is evenly doing its work across the whole surface. It is worth noting that until curing is complete, winter squash can bruise easily, despite feeling very tough, so should be handled with care.

Winter squashes can be stored until the following spring if they are kept in a cool frost-free place such as a shed, garage or porch. They should never be stored on top of each other, and a gap should be allowed between them for air to circulate. Some gardeners, if they have racks to store them on, prefer to place them stalk end down, so that no moisture or any subsequent bacteria can enter the fruit.

COMMON PROBLEMS

Mildew

The main the problem for squashes, often causing more significant issues for the summer varieties, is powdery mildew. If the white fungus takes hold on summer squashes in mid-summer, it can reduce the crop and can eventually kill the plant. It is common for it to infect plants late in the season, but is rarely an issue at this stage as it does not affect the amount or the quality of the crop. Winter squash plants can be dramatically flattened at the end of the season by mildew, but the fruit continues to ripen. The best action is prevention: make sure the soil is rich in organic matter and that the plants do not dry out once they are well established. If mildew is noticed early on a small number of leaves these can be removed (and destroyed) to slow down the spread. There are a variety of summer squashes resistant to mildew such as '*Yellow Crookneck*' and '*Defender*'.

Verticillium Wilt

This is one of many fungal problems, such as fusarium wilt that affects melons, which can cause the roots to die and the collapse of the plant. The lower leaves turn yellow first before it moves up the plant, eventually causing the leaves to turn brown and dry up. It is rare for this to be a significant problem in the UK, but young plants left sitting in cold wet soil are the most vulnerable. If it does occur, remove and destroy the plant and grow in another area the following year, or in raised beds with fresh compost.

Cucumber Mosaic Virus (CMV)

This is one of the most common viruses that affects a wide range of plants, not just cucumbers and squashes. The leaves become mottled with yellow and dark green patches and eventually become distorted. It stunts the plant's growth, reduces fruiting, and in a serious attack can cause the plant to collapse. Aphids are the biggest transmitter of the disease so they should be removed by hand or sprayed with an organic spray as soon as they are seen. It is also possible to pass on the disease from one affected plant to another by secateurs or even by hand, therefore washing of tools and hands is recommended if there is a suspicion that they have been in contact with CMV. There is no treatment other than to remove the infected parts in the hope of slowing it down. If the whole plant is affected, it should be removed and destroyed. If it is a known problem, grow varieties which are resistant such as '*Defender*'.

Leaves wilting in the sun

Squashes can, in very hot sunny weather, wilt significantly even if the soil is moist. The most common reason for this is that the plant loses water through transpiration from its large leaves quicker than it can replace it from the soil. The plant will recover when the sun goes in for a long period or overnight. If the wilting is still present the next morning it could be a fungal soil problem, but this is rare in squashes in the UK.

Slug and snail damage

Seedlings and newly planted out squashes are the most vulnerable to slug damage. Some plants at this stage can be eaten completely or the stem damaged so significantly that it will not recover. Protect using organic slug pellets or by applying nematodes. Encouraging wildlife into the garden will help with natural pest control, and carrying out nightly patrols to remove any slugs early in the season can help to reduce damage. Newly set fruits can be damaged by hungry molluscs and the easiest way to protect them is to raise them off the ground using tiles or bricks.

Blossom end rot

This is a physiological disorder rather than a disease, and therefore does not spread from one plant to another. It is caused by a lack of calcium in the young developing fruit and is most common in tomatoes, though it can also affect squashes. The fruits turn brown at the blossom end, stop growing and eventually die. It is frequently caused not so much by a lack of calcium in the soil as by the plant not being able to absorb it, which is a result of low soil pH (below 6.0), stress caused by extremes of hot or cold weather, or overly wet soil.

Fruit dying away

The main reason for embryo fruits turning brown and dying is that they have not been 'set', which is the process of pollen being transferred the from male flowers to the female ones to fertilise the fruit in order for it to grow. Plant more than one squash plant, or other flowers, to encourage pollinators to the squash flowers. If this is not successful then hand pollination (see the Pollination section for melons and watermelons for detailed instructions) is easy with squashes, as the flowers and their reproductive parts are large and the pollen is easy to see.

Growing Timeline

Mid-April to mid-May:
Sow seed either using the wet paper towel method or direct into pots and keep heated. Squashes can comfortably be left until mid-May for sowing without any detriment to growth. Once plants have filled their pots they can be potted on and grown on until planting out.

Late-May to first two weeks in June:
When the danger of frost has passed and the soil has warmed up, plant out into prepared soil. Cover with cloches or garden fleece for the first couple of weeks if available. Do not overwater.

Mid-June to end of September:
Once plants have become established and are putting on strong growth, begin feeding with liquid fertiliser and increase the watering, particularly in dry spells. Avoid wetting the crown of the plant. Hand pollinate flowers if necessary. Any fruits that set well into August should be removed, as they will not swell and ripen in time.

September to end of October:
Plant foliage will begin to die back, and the fruit will ripen and

hopefully cure in the autumn sun. If necessary, harvest fruits (with a 'T' stem attached) to cure inside when the weather turns cold or unfavourable.

October to Spring:
Enjoy the fruits fresh or store them somewhere cool, frost free and dry, and use over the winter and into spring. Research and order varieties to grow next year.

Saving Seed

Just like the other members of the cucurbit family, squashes are promiscuous and cross easily with other squashes of the same species. In general, it is agreed that *C. maxima, C. pepo, C. moschata* and *C. ficifolia* won't cross with each other. To save seed, grow them in isolation or hand pollinate. As the flowers are large they can easily be stopped from opening by using a clip or elastic band to prevent foraging pollinators potentially contaminating them with pollen. Pick out two mature male flowers to one female the day before they are expected to open, and seal them shut by tying or clipping the end of the flower. The next day, detach the male flowers and remove their petals exposing the inner parts of the flower. Gently open the female flower and rub the two male flowers on the stigma – the pollen should be visibly attached – then reseal the flower and allow the fruit to develop. Mark the fruit with a loosely tied piece of bright-coloured string so it can be identified when it is harvested. If the fruit is ripe, so will the seeds be, but curing for a couple of weeks will improve the number of viable seeds. Scoop them out into a sieve and wash them well to remove any pulp, and place them evenly on a sturdy piece of cardboard in

Pumpkin seeds

a warm room until dry. If you store them in paper envelopes or resealable plastic bags somewhere cool and dry they can remain viable for up to four years.

Being judicious about preventing cross-pollination when saving seed, particularly from summer squash (*C. pepo*), is vitally important, as rogue crosses can lead to courgettes with high levels of cucurbitacin, the chemical produced by the plant to prevent it being eaten by herbivores. When cucurbitacin is present in sufficient quantities it produces very bitter tasting fruits, which if eaten can cause digestive and other problems. If unsure, taste a small amount of the flesh, if it tastes bitter, spit it out and destroy the plant.

RECOMMENDED VARIETIES

There is a vast array of squashes to try and grow in the UK climate. This list offers a wide range of different types to search out, attempt to grow and enjoy, but is by no means definitive.

CUCURBITA PEPO

'Howden' (Heritage)
Classic ribbed orange pumpkin variety ideal for Hallowe'en carving. A reliable wide spreading plant producing multiple 10 to 14 kg fruits. Somewhat prone to mildew late in the season but this does not affect the production or ripening of fruit.

'Honey Bear' (F1) (RHS Award of Garden Merit)
An acorn shaped squash with a dark green, almost black ribbed skin with a sweet orange flesh. The fruits are an ideal size for individual servings. Compact growing habit, reliable, quick to

produce fruit, and mildew resistant makes this variety a favourite among growers.

'Honeyboat'

Arguably the sweetest squash available, and it makes an excellent replacement for butternut squash as it is much more prolific and easier to grow. The long cylindrical tanned skinned fruits have green stripes that fade when the squash is ripe. They are very versatile and can be baked, steamed, mashed or made into soups. The fruit can be eaten as soon as it is ripe or cured, and stored all winter where the sweetness remains.

'Spaghetti Squash'

An unassuming green squash that turns to orange/yellow on ripening. It comes into its own when it is cooked, as the flesh comes apart in strings like spaghetti. An excellent gluten-free and reduced carbohydrate replacement for pasta.

'Small Sugar' (Heritage Variety)

A small orange pumpkin bred for a high sugar flesh content. Ideal for soups, roasting, pies and desserts. A good choice for growing up a trellis or teepee, and in containers.

'Sweet Dumpling' (RHS Award of Garden Merit)

Small, ribbed, cream skinned fruits with green stripes and spots are produced by this interesting variety. The orange flesh is sweet with an aroma of chestnuts, and the fruits are a good size for an individual portion when stuffed and baked.

'Yellow Crookneck' (Heritage)

Dating back to the 1800s this summer squash produces curved,

'Yellow Crookneck'

club shaped fruits with a yellow skin (some varieties can also have small warts), and a slight nutty flavour. It is early and prolific, and an excellent substitute for courgettes where mildew is a problem, as it is resistant to this disease.

'Zephyr' (F1)

A unique summer squash which has yellow fruits with light green toes. The firm nutty flavoured fruits should be used like a courgette.

COURGETTES

Called zucchini in Europe and North America, courgettes are often prolific and need picking regularly before they quickly turn into marrows and stop producing. They grow in a bush habit rather than trailing long distances.

'All Green Bush' syn. *'Green Bush'*
Very popular and prolific courgette which produces good quality fruit. Aim to pick when they are between 8 to 10 cm (3 to 4 in) for optimum flavour.

'Black Beauty' syn. *'Black Milan'*, *'Nero di Milano'* (Heritage)
A traditional and popular variety with dark green, almost black shiny skin, with an excellent flavour and texture. Very reliable and productive.

'Defender' (F1) (RHS Award of Garden Merit)
A fast-growing variety that is early producing and goes on cropping until the end of the season. The plant has an open habit which makes it easy to access and pick the fruits. Resistant to powdery mildew and cucumber mosaic virus.

'Goldena' (Heritage)
Produces large crops of bright yellow courgettes with good flavour. For the best flavour aim to pick when the fruits are 10 to 15 cm (4 to 6 in) long.

'Romanesco' (Heritage) (RHS Award of Garden Merit)
Interesting heavily ribbed green fruits which have a distinct nutty flavour. The flowers are ideal for stuffing, due to being larger than other varieties.

'Ronde de Nice' syn. *'Nice à Fruit Rond'*, *'Tondo Chiaro di Nizza'*
More trailing than other courgette varieties and a vigorous grower

which has unique round fruits. Pick while the skin is still light green for best flavour.

MARROWS

Marrows are effectively courgettes that have been left to grow larger, but there are some varieties of *Cucurbita pepo* that are better suited to being grown into these sizeable fruits which can be stored. Their flesh is often not that flavourful, so they are often stuffed and baked.

'*Bush Baby*' (RHS Award of Garden Merit)
A compact variety which is suitable for small gardens or even large containers, producing small marrows up to 20 cm (8 in) in length that are easier to use in the kitchen.

'*Long Green Bush*'
Being a bush variety means that the plant remains compact and does not trail like a winter squash. It is early and heavy yielding. The fruits can be picked young and used like courgettes or allowed to grow into marrows. A favourite for exhibiting at horticultural shows.

'*Tiger Cross*' (F1) (RHS Award of Garden Merit)
A British bred and attractive looking marrow with cream stripes, which is early and prolific. '*Tiger Cross*' fruits can be picked early and used as courgettes or allowed to grow to full maturity. The plants are compact and have a good resistance to cucumber mosaic virus. They also store well when in a frost-free location. Another choice variety for showing or exhibiting at horticultural events.

'Atlantic Giant'
If the intention is to grow the largest possible pumpkin this is the variety to choose as it has held the world record since 1979. Allow at least two metres growing space between plants, and thin to one fruit. Feed and water regularly for maximum size.

'Blue Hubbard' (Heritage)
An American lantern shaped heritage variety with light blue-grey skin. Very reliable and often regarded as having one of the finest flavoured and textured fleshes, which is best baked. Stores well.

'Crown Prince' (F1) (RHS Award of Garden Merit)
A unique steel grey flat, round, ribbed winter squash with a bright

Immature 'Atlantic Giant'

orange fine-grained flesh which has a sweet, rich and nutty flavour. A reliable producer that can be stored for up to a year in optimum conditions. Rightly popular.

'*Golden Hubbard*' (Heritage)
A golden skinned variety of the '*Blue Hubbard*' with a bumpy thick skin which makes it useful for storage but difficult to peel. The orange-yellow flesh has a sweet and nutty flavour.

'*Hundredweight*'
One of the largest pumpkin varieties available. Not just a novelty as the flesh makes good quality soup and pumpkin pie. Provide at least two metres growing space per plant, add lots of compost or well-rotted manure, and thin to one fruit for maximum size.

'*Kabocha*' (F1) (RHS Award of Garden Merit)
Sometimes referred to as the Japanese pumpkin, which is not very helpful. Noted for its excellent keeping qualities, it sweetens with age. A dark green ribbed skin protects bright orange flesh which has a rich chestnut flavour. Recommended for roasting and soups.

'*Marina di Chioggia*' (Heritage)
Claims are made that this is the oldest squash variety still present in Europe, having been brought to the small fishing port of Chioggia in Italy from South America in the late 1600s. The green-grey skin is often covered in warts, and it has a bright yellow-orange flesh inside. They can be roasted, baked, or steamed, and make an excellent pie filling, but surely the most fitting is as a ravioli filling. Can be stored for up to six months.

'*Pink Banana*' (Heritage)

An American heritage variety which is a vigorous grower, producing large, long fruits which turn a pink to orange colour when ripe. The flesh is firm and sweet. An interesting variety to grow which stores well and will provoke conversation from neighbours.

'*Rouge Vif d'Etampes*' syn. '*Etamples*' (Heritage)

A lovely looking pumpkin which is sometimes referred to as the Cinderella pumpkin, the story being that this was the variety used for her carriage. Grown since at least 1830 and very popular in France, particularly around Paris. The bright orange, nearing red, knobbly skinned fruits can grow large, particularly if kept to one per plant.

'*Turk's Turban*' syn. '*Turk's Cap*' (Heritage)

A very interesting looking squash with red skin and a multicoloured growth from the blossom end, which results in the appearance of the traditional Turkish headdress. Do not be tempted to mistake it for a novelty as the flesh is nicely moist with a sweet and nutty flavour.

'*Queensland Blue*' (Heritage)

A variety from Queensland, Australia, which dates back to the early 1900s. It is a very vigorous vine which requires lots of space to grow. Bright orange flesh is contained in heavily ribbed fruits, with a typical grey/green-blue skin. Makes an excellent soup or a mash when boiled and mixed with butter.

'*Uchiki Kuri*' syn. '*Red Kuri*', '*Orange Hokkaido*' (Heritage)

Native to Japan and first grown on the island of Hokkaido. It is believed to be a descendant of a Hubbard squash and produces

'Uchiki Kuri'

'Kogigu'

3 to 5 small onion-shaped squashes per plant which have a bright orange/red skin with golden flesh. Prized for its flavour and a good size for personal use.

'Zucca da Marmellata' syn. *'Jaune Gros de Paris'* (Heritage)
An interesting flat round light orange-pink skinned squash that is low in sugar so has long been popular for making a delicious pumpkin marmalade, especially in Italy.

Cucurbita moschata

'Butternut Hunter' syn. *'Hunter'* (F1) (RHS Award of Garden Merit)
British bred so can also be grown outdoors. One of the earliest and most prolific of the butternuts for the UK climate.

'Butterbush' (F1)
A smaller bush variety producing smaller fruits that is perfect for growing in containers as well as open ground.

'Butternut Waltham' (Heritage)
A classic fine butternut type squash that has long been popular for a reason. Creamy yellow flesh with a small seed cavity. Will produce better results under cover, particularly further north.

'Kogigu' (Heritage)
An old Japanese squash producing small, dark green, almost black, ribbed and warted fruits which ripen to a lovely buff orange colour, covered in a whiteish bloom. It has a thin skin and sweet flesh, and it will prefer growing in your sunniest spot. It can take a bit of searching for the seeds, but it is worth the effort.

'*Musquée de Maroc*' (Heritage)
A striking heritage Moroccan squash which has heavily warted fruits that ripen to green and brown. Sometimes they are round, sometimes elongated like a butternut squash. Being a moschata and native to Morocco, they appreciate a greenhouse, polytunnel or plastic mulch to heat the soil. It can be a challenge to find the seeds, but it is well worth the effort to grow this unique variety. If all fails and seeds cannot be sourced, '*Zombie*' (F1) is a good modern bred alternative.

'*Musquée de Provence*' syn. '*Moschata Muscade*' '*Muscade de Provence*' (Heritage)
Attractive large flat round heavily ribbed fruits are produced by this French heritage squash. When mature, the fruit turns a golden brown, and its bright orange flesh is prized for its excellent flavour with hints of nutmeg. Stores well.

'*Tromboncino*' syn. '*Tromba d'Albenga*' (Heritage)
From the Italian coastal town of Albenga comes a unique squash producing long curved fruits. It has become a popular variety in recent years due to its ease of cultivation. The plant is best grown as a climber so that the full-length fruits can hang down. They are best harvested when green as a summer squash, though they can be allowed to mature and be stored over the winter, however they do lose flavour the more mature they get.

CUCURBITA FICIFOLIA

'*Shark Fin Melon*' syn. '*Fig Leaf Gourd*'
A squash that has acquired its most common name due to being used as a replacement for the expensive, difficult to obtain (and

controversial) shark fins that are used in the traditional Asian dish, shark fin soup. As the flesh is boiled it takes on a gelatinous texture resembling that of the shark fin. The rind isn't eaten but the flesh can be eaten raw like a cucumber. When allowed to mature on the plant, signified by the skin turning dark green and mottled with white stripes, they can be stored like winter squash, and can stay usable well into spring. They are vigorous growing plants and make an excellent annual feature when they are allowed to climb over arches, where the large fruits will hang down unsupported.

Mini cucumbers

CUCUMBERS IN THE GARDEN

Botanical information

The cucumber, *Cucumis sativus*, is a vining plant which generally produces cylindrical fruits which are most often used as a vegetable in salads, or pickled. Traditionally, cucumbers required pollination to produce fruit but they could not self-pollinate, so they needed at least two plants to be grown close together. Selective breeding created cultivars which are parthenocarpic, meaning they can produce seedless fruit without pollination. However, if pollen is allowed to be transferred from the male flowers to the female ones the fruit produced can be very bitter. Modern F1 varieties have been bred to prevent the bitterness occurring.

 Cucumbers are divided into three main categories: slicing, pickling and burpless:

Slicing are the traditional looking cucumbers, such as *'Telegraph Improved'*, which are long, thin and uniform in colour with a smooth skin. They are used fresh.

Pickling cucumbers are varieties especially selected and bred for preserving in brine and vinegar, with dill, mustard seeds and other spices. Gherkins, which are also called cornichons, are small cucumbers with warty skin that are pickled whole. Although slicing cucumbers can produce good pickles, they do not remain quite as firm as the pickling types.

Burpless varieties have become more popular in recent times as their lack of seeds and thinner skin make them more digestible than the traditional slicing cucumber. These are therefore often the varieties on offer in supermarkets.

Nutritional benefits

Cucumbers have long been regarded as a good slimming vegetable, as they are made up of about 95% water and have a very low calorie content, but recent research has shown they also contain a range of beneficial nutrients. They provide vitamin A, C and K as well as magnesium, manganese and potassium. The high water content is good for maintaining hydration and the fibre they contain can also help to maintain a good digestive system.

Requirements

Cucumbers are more robust than their melon relations, but they can still suffer from a variety of problems if their requirements are not given the respect they deserve. If you can grow melons then one or two cucumber plants – if cultivated with the same conditions and care – will provide the average family with more fruit than it can consume. As with other cucurbits, they prefer a slightly acidic soil, a pH of between 6.0 and 7.0 being the optimum range. Some types, predominantly the heritage varieties, prefer being grown under cover in a greenhouse or polytunnel, but there is a wide range of varieties that will grow and crop well outside. These are often referred to as 'ridge' cucumbers, as they were traditionally grown on ridges of soil, which prevented water sitting against the stem and risking rot. All types can be grown directly in the ground, or in containers and grow bags, but they require a fertile, free-draining compost and a full sun location. They will also be grateful of any protection that can be provided from strong winds.

Propagation

The most effective way to propagate cucumbers is to copy the method described for melons. In mid-April, for undercover growing, or late-April to early-May, for plants to be grown outside, sow one or two seeds on their side in a small pot (7 to 8 cm is ideal), cover with a small amount of compost, and top with vermiculite. Provide them with steady bottom heat and they will germinate readily. Cucumbers are not as sensitive to root shock as melons, but it is still a risk, so pricking out seedlings and potting them up should ideally be avoided. If both seedlings are required, they can be allowed to grow until roots are observed at the bottom of the pot and then both plants, along with the compost, can be removed from the pot and gently teased apart, making sure as much compost remains attached to the roots as possible. They can then be placed into individual pots, and topped up with fresh compost. Make sure the compost is moist before splitting the seedlings, as this will help to reduce root shock. Water in the new plants, and place back on the heat for the next few days until new growth is observed.

Growing Undercover

At one time growing under the protection of a greenhouse or

polytunnel was the only realistic option for cultivating quality cucumbers in northern climates. There are still many varieties which will only reliably crop with protection, and most produce long, green and smooth fruits with excellent flavour. Some of the heritage types, particularly those from warmer climates such as '*Poona Kheera*', are also best grown indoors.

Cucumbers can be grown direct in greenhouse beds on ridges, in grow bags or in large pots. If they are provided with the same treatment and conditions as melons, then they will provide a bumper crop. They will grow happily alongside tomatoes, but prefer a slightly more humid environment. They are also susceptible to stem rot and other fungal diseases, so overhead watering should be avoided at all costs. To increase the humidity and deter red spider mite damp down the floor of the indoor area in warm weather.

They can be easily trained up a single bamboo cane, on wires, using netting, or planted on top of a piece of string which runs vertically to the greenhouse frame with the central stem gently twisted around it as it grows, but they are vigorous plants and will soon reach the top of the growing space. Pruning of the stems can and should be carried out regularly to keep the plant under control. Once the main stem has reached the height required then pinch out the top to encourage side shoots. Aim to keep all side shoots to three leaves or so, or allow them to grow vertically and tie or twist them around the support. Pruning cucumbers does not create the same level of risk of disease as with melons, so carry it out freely and without worry, they grow so quickly that any mistakes will soon be rectified.

As with melons, keep them moist, but not sitting in wet soil, and do not water when the weather is cool and overcast, resume when the weather warms up again. Feed with a high potassium liquid feed once per week as soon as the flowers appear. Check the variety

MELONS & OTHER CUCURBITS

description on the seed packet and remove male flowers (the female flowers have an embryo cucumber at their base, the males do not) if told to do so to prevent bitter fruit.

Growing Outdoors

Cucumbers which are suitable for growing outside used to be referred to as 'ridge' types, as they were grown on mounds or ridges of soil to improve drainage from around the stem. At one time the quality of outdoor fruit could not rival that of the smooth, long ones grown under glass, but modern plant breeding has now provided a wide range of excellent outdoor varieties.

At least two plants should be planted to aid pollination, and they can be grown by allowing them to trail along the ground, or vertically using supports. Trailing plants should be planted 90 cm (36 in) apart with trained plants given 45 cm (18 in) between each one. To train plants vertically requires a strong support made of wood and netting or hazel sticks, as the weight of a large crop will be too much for a bamboo structure. Some growers create frames at a 45 degree angle to the sun so the plant can gain maximum sunlight and the cucumbers hang down in the shade underneath the foliage.

The site should be in full sun all day, and the ground should be prepared in advance by adding plenty of well-rotted organic material, such as garden compost or manure. If the soil can be warmed up in advance with garden fleece or black plastic then do so, as this will get the plants off to a quick start. Ideally the plants should be raised in advance and planted out once the risk of frost has passed (late-May to first week in June, depending on the area) with a slow-release fertiliser scattered on the surface around them. It is not completely necessary with the modern varieties to grow on mounds, but it is still recommended where possible. Remove the plants gently from their pots and ease into their planting holes. Do not firm in, as cucumbers are also susceptible to transplant shock. Keep water away from the stems.

FEEDING

As with all cucurbits, cucumbers grow vigorously and produce a large amount of fruit so therefore require a regular supply of the correct nutrients. If being grown outside, the initial nutrition will be provided from the organic material dug in and the slow-release fertiliser added on planting. The compost in the grow bags, and that added to the pots, will do the same. However, by the time the plant has started producing the first flowers it will require a regular boost through a liquid fertiliser high in potassium, such as tomato feed or comfrey, added weekly.

HARVESTING

It is important to harvest regularly to obtain the best tasting fruit, but also to encourage the plant to produce more cucumbers over a long season. Check the seed packet or variety list to determine the ideal size for picking the chosen variety. As a guide, small varieties should be around 10 cm (4 in) long, and large ones up to 20 cm (8 in), though they can be harvested from 10 cm (4 in) onwards. Once they have started fruiting, check them every day if possible, as they can grow rapidly. If the fruit has become bulbous or started changing colour to yellow or brown (this applies only to green varieties, others such as '*Crystal Lemon*' and '*Poona Kheera*' change colour when ripe) they have become overripe and should not be consumed as they will only deliver disappointment.

Thinning and Removing Male Flowers

Cucumbers are so prolific and crop over such a long season that it is not necessary to remove immature fruits, unless they are being grown for showing or competition. The best way to deal with the fruit is to keep eating them. However, if heritage types of cucumber are being grown they will produce male and female flowers, just like all the other cucurbits, but in the case of some cucumbers once the pollen has been transferred to the females the developing fruit becomes bitter and unpalatable. As keeping a greenhouse closed in summer is not advisable because temperatures can quickly soar, often above 40°C, and the plants suffer badly, the only realistic way to prevent pollination is to judiciously remove the male flowers before they open and make their pollen available to marauding insects. Male flowers are identified by the slim stalk behind their flower bud, while females have an embryo cucumber at the base of their flower. To lay all the cards on the table here, this is a daily endeavour, or at least every other day, as once at full steam the plants produce flowers at an amazing rate. One rogue male flower can potentially pollinate all the females open at the same time, resulting in multiple bitter cucumbers which only present themselves once they hit your tastebuds. The seed packet or website description will advise if the male flowers need to be removed. All of this, quite rightly, seems like a lot of work, and previously deterred the amateur from growing cucumbers, until better outdoor varieties and all-female flowering types were bred. However, do not let this be a barrier to the experience of growing heritage types, as there are some very special and unique cucumbers to be grown and savoured. See it as a positive daily interaction with your plants, where they can be checked and their growth observed, rather than a chore to be done. It is worth it in the end.

Cucumber Mosaic Virus (CMV)

A common disease in cucumbers which can destroy a whole crop. The first signs of the problem are that the leaves become mottled with yellow and dark green patches, followed by the leaf surface becoming distorted. It causes stunting of the plant growth and in severe infections the whole plant can collapse. Its spread can be slowed down by pruning off infected leaves, but all material removed should be destroyed by burning. Sanitise any tools that have had contact with the plants.

Mildew

A fungal disease affecting the plant's leaves and reducing its vigour. It is mainly caused by dry soil and a humid atmosphere, and manifests itself in a white powdery coating over the upper surface of the leaves. The best prevention is to keep the soil moist, and keep under cover growing areas well ventilated in warm weather.

Stem Rot

Cucumbers, like other cucurbits, are at risk of stem rot. Dust with yellow sulphur where necessary and keep water away from the stems. More detailed information is described in the melon growing section.

Anthracnose and Verticillium Wilt

Two fungal diseases which affect the leaves of all cucurbits but are not commonly problematic in cucumbers. They are also detailed in the melon growing section.

Red Spider Mite

A common problem in hot dry indoor growing environments. The first sign of an infection is very fine webbing around leaves. As the infection gets worse the leaves become speckled and turn yellow, and eventually the whole plant becomes stunted and fails. Red spider mites dislike humid environments, so damp down regularly in hot spells (sometimes multiple times per day) but never apply water directly to the leaves.

Bitter Flavoured Cucumbers

Mainly an issue with varieties that need to be grown under cover, and some heritage varieties. With these types it is caused by the female flowers being pollinated by insects transferring pollen from the male flowers. To prevent this, all the male flowers should be removed as soon as they appear. Other causes can be sudden changes in weather from cold to hot, or erratic watering regimes. Keep the compost lightly moist and ventilate well on hot days to reduce the temperature.

Growing Timeline

Mid-April to mid-May:

Sow seed either using the wet paper towel method, or directly into pots, and keep heated. Varieties to be grown under cover should be started mid to late April and the ones planned for outdoor growing saved until early to mid-May. Prick out seedlings individually into 7 to 8 cm pots, and grow on indoors protecting them from frost.

Mid-May to first two weeks in June

Plants to be grown in a greenhouse or polytunnel can be planted into their final positions in mid-May if the weather conditions are favourable and set fair until the end of the month. If not, leave until the end of May. At the end of May, the first couple of weeks in June, or as soon as the risk of frost has passed, plant out outdoor varieties.

If the frost risk has gone, but the weather is cool and wet, wait until the weather warms up before planting out.

Mid-June to end of September:
Once plants have become established and are commencing flowering start to feed with a high potassium liquid fertiliser, and keep the compost moist. Remove male flowers before they open on varieties that can pollinate and produce bitter fruits. Pick fruits as soon as they are ready, as this will encourage the plant to continue cropping.

September to end of October:
Keep harvesting and enjoying the fruits. Mildew will undoubtably set in as the nights become cooler, but at this stage it will not have any effect on the cropping. As the plants start to die harvest all fruits, and if there are too many to eat give them away or pickle them for winter use.

SAVING SEED

Cucumbers, *C. sativus*, like other cucurbits, will cross-pollinate with others of the same species, but will not with other members of the genus, such as melons, watermelons and squash. Therefore, cucumbers for seed saving should either be grown in isolation (which is generally the easiest method for cucumbers) or hand pollinated as described in the Pollination section for melons. A large amount of the modern cucumber varieties are F1 hybrids, which means the seed will never come true (produce the same variety it was harvested from), so seed should not be saved from them.

If seed of heritage varieties is to be saved, then stop removing the male flowers to allow the pollen to be transferred to the females, which will then form seeds. Let insects carry out this process or do it by hand. Let the fruits mature completely, which is usually signified

MELONS & OTHER CUCURBITS

by the skin turning yellow or brown, then cut open the fruit and scoop out the seed from the central cavity with a spoon. The seed is covered in a gelatinous coating which ideally needs to be removed to improve germination. The best method of doing this is to place the seeds and attached coating into a glass or bowl of water, and allow to ferment for three days. Stir at least once every day, but do not let it ferment for longer, as the seeds can germinate in the water. After three days pour off as much of the water as you can without losing any seeds that have sunk to the bottom. The liquid will contain debris and floating seeds which should be discarded. Fill the container halfway with clean water, stir, let the seeds settle and pour off the liquid and repeat this process until the liquid comes out clear and the seeds are clean. Place the cleaned seeds on a piece of cardboard and dry in a warm place out of direct sun. Once they are dry, place them in sealed plastic bags or paper envelopes, and store somewhere cool and dry. Ideally use within five years of harvesting.

RECOMMENDED VARIETIES

'Burpless Tasty' (F1)
Arguably the best cucumber for outdoor growing in northern climates. Produces crisp fruits with no bitterness which are easy to digest.

'Bush Champion' (F1)
A compact bush variety producing up to 20 cm (8 in) long cucumbers. A good choice for container growing and outside in a sunny spot. Shows some resistance to cucumber mosaic virus.

'Carmen' (F1) (RHS Award of Garden Merit)
An excellent modern all-female flowering hybrid of the traditional,

smooth, long, slicing cucumber. The never bitter fruits can be up to 40 cm (16 in) in length and the plants are cold-tolerant, so will produce an earlier crop. A good choice for exhibiting but the seeds are expensive to buy.

'*Crystal Lemon*' (Heritage)

A unique cucumber resembling a cross between a lemon and a melon with particularly spikey stems. Can be slow to come into fruit compared to other cucumbers but is then prolific, particularly if you keep picking them from golf ball to tennis ball sized. The prickles also extend to the skin of the fruit, so it is best pealed before eating. Don't let this put you off, as the sweet crisp flesh has no bitter taste and claims to be more digestible than traditional cucumbers. Also suitable for outdoor growing.

'*La Diva*' (F1)

An excellent hybrid outdoor all-female flowering outdoor variety which can also be cultivated under cover for earlier fruiting. The fruits are smooth, with the traditional cucumber flavour of indoor types. Harvest the never bitter fruits from the size of a gherkin onwards. Demonstrates excellent resistance to powdery and downy mildew.

'*Marketmore*' (RHS Award of Garden Merit)

A classic tasting outdoor cucumber with slightly bumpy straight green-fleshed fruits which can grow up to 20 cm (8 in) long. The plants show resistance to mildew.

'*Mini Munch*' (F1) (RHS Award of Garden Merit)

A compact variety which prolifically produces snack-sized fruits up to 10 cm (4 in) in length, with excellent flavour. Well suited to outdoor and container growing. Resistant to powdery mildew.

'*Crystal Lemon*' cucumber

'*Poona Kheera*' (Heritage)
An Indian cucumber variety which starts out lime green and turns orange when mature, but the very crisp fruits can be eaten at any stage. Will definitely generate interest from other growers. Better suited for greenhouse cultivation.

'*Telegraph Improved*' (Heritage) (RHS Award of Garden Merit)
An 'improved' variety of the original '*Telegraph*' cucumber which was introduced in 1897. Classic, long, smooth skinned and crunchy fruits. A favourite of show gardeners and one to try if you want to match the ruler-straight cucumbers of Victorian estate gardeners. Best suited for greenhouse cultivation. Remove any male flowers which appear before they can open.

'*White Wonder*' syn. '*Bianco Lungo*' (Heritage)
A prolific small white cucumber originally offered by an American seed company in 1890. The ivory white fruits are excellent for slicing, with a hint of citrus flavour. Will grow outdoors in the UK.

Gherkins

Also known as 'pickling cucumbers', these are small warty cucumbers that are best suited to pickling rather than slicing for salads.

'*Diamant*' (F1)
A heavy cropping and very early variety which produces very firm fruits ideal for pickling whole. An excellent choice for outdoor growing which shows good resistance to disease.

'*Parisian Pickling*' syn. '*National*' (Heritage)
Dating back to 1876, this variety has dark green skin with firm thick

flesh that is perfect for pickling. Seeds are very small when fruits are picked young. Rub off any small prickles that are present on the skin before using.

'White Pickle Mini' (Heritage)

An interesting white pickling cucumber. Very prolific and compact plant which is ideal for containers. Pickle when fruits are less than 8 cm (3 ½ in) long, if allowed to grow bigger they are good to use as slicing cucumbers.

Winter Squash

OTHER CUCURBITS TO CONSIDER GROWING

Luffa

Luffa is a genus of cucurbit from tropical and sub-tropical climates whose name derives from '*Lūf*' in Egyptian Arabic. They can be eaten raw or cooked like squash when immature and are popular in Asian cuisine. Once they are allowed to mature and dry they can be used as an exfoliating sponge, which is then commonly, and confusingly called a 'loofah'. There are three species of luffa but the two to be concerned with for short season climates are *Luffa actuangula* and *L. cylindrica* (also sometimes called *L. aegyptiaca*). Both will produce sponges but if they are also to be eaten then choose *L. actuangula* as the flavour is reputed to be better than that of the cylindrical type.

They are very vigorous growers and will grow outside in a sunny protected site but for a guaranteed crop grow them under cover. Grow as per instructions for cucumbers and start them on heat (ideally between 25 to 30°C) in April, as per melons. Sow more seeds than you require as germination is erratic and can take up to 21 days. Prick them out into 7 to 10 cm (3 to 4 in) pots and grow on before planting under cover in late May, or outside after the frost has passed. If growing in containers, aim for a 30 to 45 cm (12 to 16 in) pot or two plants per grow bag. A strong support is required and plants will need to be tied in regularly to keep them organised. They can make an attractive and conversation-provoking feature if planted either side of an arch and trained to climb over, and the long fruits will hang down inside the arch.

If they are to be harvested for eating, then pick before they reach 10 cm (4 in) long. Picking will encourage more fruit production. If the aim is to produce a loofah, then leave the fruit on the plant to mature. As it does so, the skin hardens and turns from green to yellow and then brown. Harvest when yellow for a light-coloured sponge or allow to turn all the way brown for a dark-coloured one. If the weather is turning poor quickly and there is a risk it will not ripen on the vine, then the fruit which has started to turn yellow can be brought inside, placed somewhere warm and dry, and it will often ripen to brown and dry out completely.

To obtain the sponge, the mature fruit needs to be cut from the plant and the skin removed. There are two main ways to do this, the first is to crack open the skin and peel it off. The skin and loofah inside are very tough, so the fruit can be thrown against a solid floor or wall outside (a technique for both the young and old to enjoy) to crack open the skin, which is then peeled off. Start at the blossom end and shake out the seeds into a container for growing next year. It is recommended to wear gloves and to do this outside, as shards of fruit covering can break the skin, and it can also be very dusty. The fruit skin does not always come away easily, and if this (and the dust) is a problem then submerge the fruit in a bucket of water for 24 to 48 hours, remove and drain, and the skin should come away easier. If any flesh or debris remains in the loofah then soak it again for a day or so and rinse clean. Use whole or cut up into smaller sections as an exfoliating sponge when bathing, or as an abrasive

MELONS & OTHER CUCURBITS

sponge when washing up. Harvested seeds should be dried out on cardboard as per melons and watermelons.

Cucamelon or Mouse Melon

Cucamelon, *Melothria scabra*, is a species of cucurbit native to Central America from Mexico to Venezuela, where it is known locally as '*Sandiitas de Raton*' or simply '*Sandiita*'. It is grown for its very small fruits, which taste similar to cucumber but with a citrus kick. They can be eaten raw, used in salads and salsa, or pickled whole like gherkins. Once pickled they make an excellent accompaniment to olives for tapas. They also add interest and flavour to a gin and tonic or a cocktail when used as a garnish.

They can be grown inside or outside, but, as ever, results are better under cover. Follow the methods for growing melons or cucumbers, and train up a similar structure. They are free from major pests and diseases and tolerate drought well. The plants are vigorous and once they reach the apex of the indoor growing space, or about 2.5 m (8 ft), then pinch out the top of the plant to encourage side shoots. Prune back side shoots to 40 cm (16 in) in length. The fruiting season is from July until September and fruits should be harvested when they are the size of grapes and still firm. If they are left any longer the flavour and texture deteriorate quickly and significantly. As with other cucurbits they are frost sensitive, but cucamelons are perennial and, once the fruiting season is over and before the first frost, the plant can be cut back and the roots lifted and stored in a dark frost-free place (such as a garage or shed) in just-moist compost. On the dry side is better than wet. The root can be potted up in March or early April and will regrow. Grow on in a frost-free place and plant out again in late May to early June, and the plant will produce and crop earlier than if grown from seed.

Bitter Melon

Momordica charantia, the bitter melon or bitter gourd, is native to the tropical areas of south Asia and is believed to have made its way to China, in the fifteen or sixteenth century, and then onto Japan, where it is called '*gōyā*' and is a popular cooking and medicinal ingredient, particularly around Okinawa.

In recent years the health benefits of bitter melons have been studied, and they have been found to contain a range of antioxidants. Indeed, eating them has been linked to helping reduce blood sugar and cholesterol. A juice made from the fruit, known as karela juice, is believed to help the liver and digestive system, and to promote skin health.

A vigorous vining plant, bitter melon grows bumpy cylindrical fruit in a similar way to cucumbers. As the plant is native to tropical areas, in its short season in northern climates it should be grown under the protection of a polytunnel or greenhouse. The seeds have a hard coat and germination rates can be improved by soaking them overnight in water before sowing. Sow seeds as per cucumbers and try to maintain a bottom heat of 20 to 25°C. Prick out into 7 to 10 cm (3 to 4 in) pots and grow on until mid-May when, if weather conditions permit, they should be planted into their final growing positions 50 cm (20 in) apart in beds, two plants per grow bag, or one plant per 30 to 45 cm (12 to 18 in) pot filled with good quality compost. Plants should be supported by canes or netting, and tied in regularly, nipping out the growing tip once it reaches the top of the growing area, with side shoots being kept to approximately 40 cm (16 in) long. Once flowers appear, feed with a high potassium liquid feed and hand pollinate as per melons if insects are not noticeably visiting the plants.

Harvest the fruits when they have grown to at least 5 cm (2 in) long. The darker skinned varieties are the most bitter, but they can be lightly peeled to reduce their pungency if required. They are very bitter when raw, so they should be sprinkled with salt (or bathed in salt water) for at least 20 minutes to extract some of the bitter juices. The white varieties do not need salting and can be tried raw. A classic way to eat them is to slice them open, remove the inner flesh and seeds, salt them, and then stuff them with cooked spiced potatoes and onions. The stuffed fruit is then coated with flour and lightly fried, similar to a samosa. The fruit is also widely used in stir fries and soups.

Kiwano, the African Horned Melon

A real curiosity of the cucurbit family, *Cucumis metuliferus*, kiwano, also known as the blowfish melon, is a plant native to Africa and produces very spikey orange fruit. The green seed containing pulp is eaten fresh like a passion fruit (the seeds are edible) and has a tart taste of cucumber, banana and citrus. The peel is also eaten in Africa, and is rich in fibre and vitamin C.

The plants require warmth so should be grown under cover, but be warned, they are very vigorous growers and can take over a greenhouse unless controlled by judicious pruning. Support them with canes and trellis. Grow as per melons, germinating on bottom heat between 20 and 30°C. Prick out, grow on and plant in their final positions in 30 to 45 cm (12 to 18 in) pots filled with good compost, two plants to a grow bag, or direct into indoor growing beds with a good helping of organic material worked in. Feed with a high potassium liquid feed when flowers start to appear, and hand pollinate if insects are not noticed to be visiting the flowers. The fruits can be harvested and eaten at any stage of ripening (indicated by a change in the colour from green to orange).

Cantaloupe melon

CUCURBITS IN THE KITCHEN

SHARK FIN MELON SOUP

An alternative to the traditional and controversial shark fin soup using the flesh of the shark fin melon. As the melon boils it separates and creates a gelatinous texture similar to that of the shark fin. You can play around with adding other root vegetables or Asian ingredients you like but this is a good easy base recipe.

Ingredients:
1 kg (2 ¼ lb) (approx) shark fin melon flesh, cut into pieces
3 carrots, peeled and chopped into small chunks
2 tomatoes chopped (optional)
dried mushrooms or mushroom powder (whichever you prefer)
dried chilli flakes

Add the shark fin melon and carrot pieces to a large pan and cover with enough water so that there is approximately 1 cm (½ in) above the ingredients. Bring to the boil, reduce to a simmer and cover until they are tender.

Add the chopped tomatoes (if using) and dried mushrooms and simmer for another five minutes or until the mushrooms are soft. If you are using mushroom powder stir in a teaspoon at the end. Season with chilli flakes, salt and pepper and mix well to make sure the shark fin melon has broken down and is distributed throughout the soup. The carrots, mushrooms and tomatoes should remain whole. Serve piping hot.

Watermelon Gazpacho

A twist on the traditional Spanish tomato gazpacho by 'Great British Chefs' which is perfect for those hot August days.

Ingredients:
500 g (18 oz) cherry or baby Roma tomatoes, halved
500 g (18 oz) watermelon, cut into chunks, seeds removed
½ cucumber, peeled and roughly chopped
5 to 6 tbsp olive oil,
1 to 2 tbsp red wine vinegar
1 slice of stale bread, white, broken into pieces
2 or 3 garlic cloves, crushed
salt and pepper to taste

Put the tomato, watermelon, cucumber and stale bread in a blender and blitz, adding pieces of garlic one at a time, and taste after each addition to determine the level of garlic flavour you desire.

Add the olive oil and vinegar, and blend until smooth and creamy. It might be necessary to separate into batches if it does not fit into your blender. A stick blender will probably not attain the consistency required. Season with salt and pepper and place in the fridge to chill for at least one hour. Serve with a sprinkling of grated cucumber.

Stuffed Courgette Flowers

This recipe, inspired by one on the BBC Good Food website, can be a little tricky when it comes to stuffing the flowers with the filling but this classic Mediterranean dish is a delight to eat and looks great on the plate. The goat's cheese adds depth of flavour but the dish can also be made using only ricotta.

Ingredients:
8 courgette flowers, with small courgette attached
sunflower oil

For the batter:
1 large egg
100 g (3 ½ oz) plain flour
pinch of bicarbonate of soda
200 ml (½ pint) iced water

For the filling:
250 g (9 oz) ricotta (you may not need all of this)
150 g (5 oz) soft goat's cheese
zest of 1 lemon
½ red chilli, finely chopped (if desired)
30 g (1 oz) pine nuts, chopped (if desired for flavour and texture)
a small handful mint, coriander or parsley leaves, chopped (or a
  mixture based on your taste)

Make the batter by whisking the flour, egg and bicarbonate of soda in a bowl. Add the iced water a little at a time while continuing to whisk until the batter is smooth and the consistency of double cream.

In another bowl mix all the filling ingredients together until well combined, and finish with a pinch of salt and pepper worked in.

As carefully as you can, open up the flower and remove the stamen if present. Spoon the prepared filling mix into the flower as gently as possible, and don't be tempted to overfill it. Close the flower by twisting the ends of the petals together.

Dip the flowers in the batter, ensuring they are evenly coated, and fry them until crisp. If you have a deep-fryer, set it to 180°C, if not, you can shallow fry the flowers in a pan for two minutes each side, being careful not to damage them when you turn them over. Once fried, remove the flowers and drain on kitchen paper before seasoning with salt. Serve on their own, with a dip or as a side dish.

Roasted Squash

Roasted squash makes the basis of many of recipes, so it is useful to know the technique to achieve the best quality result.

Always overestimate by up to 100 g (3 ½ oz) the amount required to account for the skin and weight lost in moisture as it cooks.

Cut the required weight of squash into approximately 4 cm (1 ½ in) squares, leaving the skin on. Place the squares skin side down onto a baking sheet and cover tightly with foil. Roast in a pre-heated oven at 220°C / 200°C fan / gas mark 7 for 25 minutes or until soft (which can be tested with a sharp knife). Take out of the oven, remove the foil and allow to cool for most recipes.

Indian Stuffed Crispy Bitter Melons

A popular way to cook bitter melons in south Asia is to stuff them with a spiced mix of vegetables and lightly fry them like a samosa. Alternatively, they can be filled with a soft cheese mix, similar to jalapeño 'poppers' (stuffed jalapeño peppers). This recipe was inspired and adapted from one published on the Veganlovlie website.

Ingredients:
For the marinade:
5 medium sized bitter melons
2 tsp salt

For the samosa-style filling:
1 large potato chopped into 1.5 cm (½ in) cubes
½ medium onion, finely chopped
50 g (1 ¾ oz) carrot, finely diced
50g (1 ¾ oz) frozen peas
1 tbsp vegetable oil
1 to 2 tsp of curry powder or your own curry spice mix
fresh coriander leaves
salt to taste

* for an alternative filling 100 to 150 g (4 to 5 oz) of cream cheese
   will be needed

For the coating:
5 to 10 cm (2 to 4 in) long coriander stems with leaves removed,
   or cooking string
70 g (2 ½ oz) chickpea flour or any other all-purpose flour
cooking oil for shallow frying

Remove some of the outer skin by lightly scraping with a knife or peeler and make a slit along the length and scoop out the seeds. Place the prepared bitter melons in a bowl and sprinkle with the salt. Rub the salt into the skin and then cover with water and soak for at least 20 minutes.

Prepare the samosa-style filling by lightly frying the onions in ½ tablespoon of oil in a pan. Add the curry power then add the carrots and potatoes, along with a touch of salt and a little water (you can always add more) to help soften the potatoes. Stir well and cover with a lid or baking foil, and cook on a medium heat until the potatoes are soft, which should take 12 to 15 minutes. Stir occasionally and add more water if required to keep the mixture moist but not wet.

When the potatoes feel soft (test by pushing a knife into them and if it goes in without resistance they are ready), mash them, and then place back on the heat for a couple of minutes. Add the coriander leaves and turn off the heat. Skip this step if you prefer to stuff the bitter melons with cream cheese.

If you wish to use the coriander stems to tie the bitter melons together rather than using cooking string, you need to lightly cook them to make them flexible. Place the stems in a saucepan and cover with cold water. Bring to the boil for a couple of minutes then remove and place in a bowl of cold water to stop them from cooking any further.

Take the bitter melons and rinse in cold water to remove the salt and some of the bitterness. Stuff the chosen filling into each fruit carefully using a teaspoon, without overfilling. Tie each bitter melon with the coriander stems or cooking string to stop the filling coming out when frying, then roll each of the melons in some chickpea flour. Coat them well in the flour, tapping to remove the excess.

Heat a pan to a medium to high temperature and add two tablespoons of vegetable oil and shallow fry the prepared bitter melons. Turn them regularly to ensure that they are evenly fried. Once they turn golden-brown and crispy, remove them from the pan and drain on absorbent paper. Serve them as a snack or as a main with rice and roti. Alternatively, you can use them as a side dish to many curry dishes.

MELONS & OTHER CUCURBITS

Pumpkin Ravioli with Sage Butter

Tortelli di zucca is a classic northern Italian pasta dish from the Emilia-Romagna region which is traditionally served with a sage butter sauce on special occasions such as Christmas eve. This recipe is adapted from one by Rick Stein, which appeared in *Gardeners' World* magazine.

Ingredients:
For the filling:
450 g (16 oz) pumpkin
1 tbsp olive oil
large pinch of crushed fennel seeds
1 medium egg yolk
25 g (¾ oz) grated parmesan cheese, plus extra to serve
pinch of grated nutmeg
2 amaretti biscuits, crushed
15 g (½ oz) white breadcrumbs
salt and black pepper

For the egg pasta:
225 g (8 oz) plain flour
¼ tsp salt
½ tsp olive oil
2 medium eggs
4 medium egg yolks
rocket leaves to serve (optional)

For the sage butter:
75 g (2 ½ oz) unsalted butter
20 small sage leaves
1 tbsp lemon juice

Preheat the oven to 220ºC / 200ºC fan / gas mark 7 and cut the pumpkin into wedges and scoop out the seeds, leaving the skin on. Place in a roasting tin and sprinkle with oil, fennel seeds, salt and pepper. Mix to make sure as much of the pumpkin is coated, and roast for 30 minutes until tender. Remove from the oven and leave until cool, then scoop the flesh away from the skin.

While the pumpkin cools make the pasta dough by blending all the ingredients in a food processor until they come together in a ball. Knead the dough on a flour dusted work surface until smooth, cut in half and roll into two balls. Wrap both in cling film and allow to rest at room temperature for approximately 30 minutes.

Make a purée from the cooled pumpkin by placing it in a bowl and mashing with a fork. Add the egg yolk, parmesan, nutmeg, amaretti biscuits, breadcrumbs and a little salt and pepper, and stir until well combined.

Bring a large pan of salted water (roughly one teaspoon of salt to 600 ml of water) to the boil then make the ravioli by taking one ball of the dough and rolling it out to 2 mm (just under ⅛ in) thick. If using a pasta machine work down to setting number 5. Lay the sheet on a flat, lightly floured surface and cut out circles using a 12 cm (5 in) cutter. Working quickly place a teaspoon of the filling into the middle of each circle. Brush any visible pasta with water and fold over the filling into a half moon shape. Gently press around the filling to release any air and seal the ravioli. Repeat with the second ball of dough and cook the ravioli in the boiling water for 2 to 4 minutes, remove and drain.

To make the sage butter sauce, melt the butter in a large frying pan until foaming and put in the sage and fry for a few seconds. Remove the pan from the heat and add the lemon juice, salt and pepper. Place the ravioli in a bowl, either on its own or on a light bed of rocket leaves, pour the sage butter over the pasta and top with grated parmesan and serve immediately.

Pumpkin Pie

The traditional seasonal dessert at harvest time across the US. The sweeter varieties of pumpkin such as '*Musquée de Provence*', '*Howden*' or '*Small Sugar*' are excellent choices for this recipe, which is derived from one printed by the National Trust in its members magazine.

Ingredients:
For the pastry:
150 g (5 oz) butter, chilled
250 g (9 oz) plain flour plus extra for rolling out
1 medium egg
pinch of salt

For the filling:
650 g (23 oz) (before cooking) pumpkin roasted and cooled (as
  per the 'Roasted Squash' instructions)
¼ tsp ground nutmeg*
¼ tsp ground ginger*
¼ tsp ground cinnamon*
* note: these three spices can be replaced by ¾ tsp of mixed spice
  or pumpkin spice mix
75 g (2 ½ oz) light brown sugar or 75 ml (¼ pint) maple syrup
3 large eggs, beaten
200 ml (8 oz) double cream

Mix the flour and salt in a bowl, cut the butter into small pieces and rub it into the mix with your fingertips until it resembles breadcrumbs. Slowly add the egg and mix well with a spoon or spatula to form a dough. Make the dough into a ball and wrap in cling film. Place in the fridge for at least 30 minutes.

Pre-heat the oven to 220ºC / 200ºC fan / gas mark 7 and roll out the pastry to about the thickness of a pound coin. Grease a 22 cm (9 in) loose-bottomed tart tin and line with the pastry, prick over the base with a fork, line with baking paper and fill with baking beans. Bake for about 20 minutes then remove the paper and beans and allow the pastry to cool fully.

Turn the oven down to 200ºC / 180ºC fan / gas mark 6. Blend

Melon with Orange and Elderflower

or mash the cooled pumpkin (it must be completely cooled or it will cook the egg before it gets to the oven) until smooth and add the spices, sugar and eggs, then finally the double cream. Mix well to combine all the ingredients.

Pour the filling into the cooled pastry case and bake for about 40 minutes until it has just set. Leave to cool in the tin where it will set further. Enjoy on its own or with cream.

Melon with Orange, Elderflower and Herbs

Ingredients (serves 4):
6 bushy sprigs of mint
4 sprigs of marjoram or basil
750 ml (1 ½ pint) elderflower cordial in water
1 orange
1 ripe cantaloupe melon, 1.5 kg (3 ½ lb) although you may not
  need all of it

Make the elderflower cordial, strength according to taste. If you have homemade elderflower cordial, of course use that.

Halve the melon, scoop out any seeds and any core. Cut the melon flesh into pieces and add enough diluted elderflower cordial to give a good flavour. Remove the peel from the orange, take out any pith and seeds, and cut into juicy segments. Then add the orange segments to the melon and elderflower cordial. Next add the mint, basil, or marjoram. If you wish, crush some of the herbs a little and steep them in the elderflower cordial to add an intensified flavour.

Place the melon and orange, steeped in the cordial, into a bowl and sprinkle the herb leaves on the fruit.

(The inspiration for this recipe came from Nigel Slater's Melon with Mint and Basil).

Butternut Squash and White Chocolate Crème Brûlée

Ingredients (for 6 small pots of crème brûlée)
300 ml (⅔ pint) double cream
1 vanilla pod
50 g (1 ¾ oz) or 2 slices of butternut squash
3 large egg yolks (discard the whites)
1-2 tablespoons of golden caster sugar
60 g (2 oz) white chocolate (Lindt or similar)

Heat oven to 160°C or gas mark 4. Boil the butternut squash in hot water for about 10 minutes until soft. Put the double cream in a saucepan, and gently heat along with the white chocolate, stirring all the time. Add the vanilla seeds which you extract from the vanilla pod with a sharp knife, or your fingers, if the tiny seeds are moist and fresh. When the chocolate has melted, take the pan off the heat and let it cool for 10 minutes. Be sure not to boil the cream. Add the cooked butternut squash, and mix it thoroughly with a spoon until it is not really visible.

In a separate bowl, add the 3 egg yolks, having carefully discarded the whites, and mix in a generous tablespoon of the golden caster sugar. Add the cooled cream and white chocolate.

Pour the custard into six ramekins. Stand them in a roasting tin which has been filled with hot, recently boiled water three-quarters of the way up the sides of the ramekins. Transfer, and cook in the oven for 30 to 40 minutes, until just set and with a skin formed. Leave to cool and chill in the fridge. Then add the rest of the golden caster sugar, and use a blowtorch to caramelise the sugar, which only takes about 3 seconds. Be careful not to burn the sugar. If you do not have a blowtorch you can caramelise the sugar under the grill.

Serve within an hour so the sugar is still a crunchy topping. Decorate with a fresh raspberry or mint leaves if you wish.

MELONS & OTHER CUCURBITS

Butternut Squash Crème Brûlée

Spiced Pumpkin Scones

Spiced Pumpkin Scones

An autumnal twist on the classic British scone from BBC Good Food. Serve buttered or with cream cheese.

Ingredients:
450 g (16 oz) self-raising flour, plus extra for rolling
100 g (3 ½ oz) cold butter
50 g (1 ¾ oz) golden caster sugar (add a little more if you prefer them sweeter)
1 to 2 tsp pumpkin spice (or mix ½ tsp cinnamon, ¼ tsp ginger, a good grind of nutmeg and a pinch of allspice).
200 g (7 oz) cooked or roasted pumpkin, cooled
80-100 ml (¼ pint) milk (can be substituted for a non-dairy alternative)
butter or cream cheese to serve

Heat oven to 220ºC / 200ºC fan / gas mark 7. Put the flour in a bowl and coarsely grate in the butter (dipping the butter into the flour can make it easier to grate; do this as often as you need). Use a butter knife to stir the butter into the flour, then mix in the sugar and spice.

Add the pumpkin and 80 ml milk to the flour mixture and quickly stir everything together. Add more milk if you need to.

Tip the mixture onto a floured surface and lightly bring together with your hands a couple of times. Roll out until 4 cm (1 ½ in) thick and stamp out rounds with a 7 cm (3 in) cutter. Reshape the trimmings until all the dough has been used. Place the rounds on a lightly buttered or oiled baking sheet and brush the tops with any remaining milk. Bake for 10 to 12 minutes until they have risen and are lightly browned.

Pumpkin Marmalade

This traditional Italian preserve, called Zucca da Marmellata, can be made from any sweet winter squash but to stay true to its history use the variety carrying the same name. The recipe has been adapted from one published by Riverford Organic Farmers.

Ingredients:
500 g (18 oz) winter squash or pumpkin flesh (skin and seeds removed)
500g (18 oz) granulated sugar
1 orange
125 ml (¼ pint) water

Pumpkin Marmalade

The measurements can be scaled up or down depending on the amount of marmalade you want to make.

Cut the squash into small cubes and mix with sugar in a large bowl and cover with cling film. Slice the oranges thinly and cut slices into quarters. Place in a different bowl to the squash and add the water. Also cover with cling film and leave both bowls to stand for 24 hours, stirring the squash mix occasionally.

Put the oranges and the now-infused water into a large saucepan and bring to the boil. Add the squash and sugar mix and bring back to a gentle boil while stirring regularly to dissolve the sugar. Reduce the heat to simmer for 30 to 45 minutes until the mixture is thick and syrupy and comes away from the pan easily when stirred. Pour into sterilised jars and seal.

Watermelon Jam

A great way to use up excess watermelon and preserve that summer flavour all winter long in a jam that you will not find on the supermarket shelves. As watermelons do not contain pectin this needs to be added in order for the jam to set. The quantities can easily be scaled up or down depending on the amount of watermelon available or jam you want to make. Adapted from a recipe kindly shared by Melanie Mendelson on her 'Melanie Cooks' website.

Ingredients:
400 g (14 oz) watermelon, seeds removed and pureed
400 g (14 oz) white sugar
60 ml (⅛ pint) of fresh lemon juice
pectin (follow instructions on packaging for quantity required)

Add the puréed watermelon, lemon juice and sugar to a metal pan suitable for jam making. Bring to a rolling boil, then reduce heat to simmer.

Add the pectin and immediately whisk it with a handheld whisk or a fork, ensuring it dissolves completeely, without clumping. Bring the jam to a boil again, and then reduce heat to simmer, stirring every minute, for about 20 minutes.

Pour the jam into sterilised jars and seal while still hot. Allow to cool and set.

Lacto-Fermented Watermelon Rind Pickle

A modern twist on the traditional pickled watermelon rind using lacto-fermentation. This is a process which has been carried out for centuries but has come back into vogue recently due to its health benefits. The process involves fermenting vegetables in brine; the salt preventing 'bad', food-spoiling bacteria from developing, and the 'good' lactobacillus bacteria converting sugars in the vegetables into lactic acid, which preserves the food and gives it a unique tangy flavour. There are many potential benefits, including adding these bacteria to the digestive system and the fermentation process releasing more of the vegetables' nutrients, while at the same time making them more digestible.

These pickles make an excellent side to Japanese and Korean dishes, but are equally at home served with strong cheeses, such as cheddar, or as an interesting replacement for sauerkraut.

Ingredients:
enough watermelon rind to fill a 500 ml (1 pint) jar or
  fermenter (approx half a watermelon)
200 g (7 oz) filtered water
6 g (¼ oz) sea salt or pure salt (not table salt or other versions

with additives)
*½ tsp dried mustard seeds**
*½ tsp dried fennel**
* *the mustard and fennel can be replaced with a pickling spice*
  mix or you could make your own)

For this recipe a 3% salt brine is required. The easiest way to do this is to weigh out 200 g (7 oz) of water in a jug and stir in 6 g (.2 oz) of sea salt until dissolved. Leave until the rinds are ready.

Open the watermelon and cut out all the flesh from the white rind. A thin layer of flesh can be left on the rind to add colour to the pickle. Peel all the green or yellow skin from the rind and chop into 2 cm (¾ in) squares. Add the dried mustard seeds and fennel to the jar or fermenter, and then fill with the watermelon rind squares to approximately 3 cm (1 ¼ in) from the neck of the vessel. Gently pour the brine over the rind until there is enough to cover the rind.

The rind needs to be submerged throughout the fermentation process. Purpose-made fermentation weights can be bought but a sterilised jam jar lid will achieve this if it is gently submerged with the lid top facing down. Some of the brine will flow into the lid thread recess and create enough weight to keep the rind from breaking the surface. Cover the top with an air lock, lid or cling film held in place with an elastic band.

As the lactobacillus gets to work it will give off carbon dioxide which will be seen as bubbles rising to the surface of the brine. If an airlock is not being used the top should be opened briefly every two days to release this gas and then re-sealed.

Leave at room temperature for four or five days, at which point it will be ready to eat. Move to the refrigerator to slow down or stop the fermentation process.

Melon and Thyme Pickle with White Balsamic Vinegar

Ingredients:
2 large slices of a ripe, sweet canteloupe melon
½ tsp table salt
6 tbsp white balsamic vinegar
15 or so black peppercorns
lemon thyme sprigs (any other type of thyme will do, but lemon
*   thyme tends not to have hard stems that you need to remove)*

Choose a sweet melon, for example canteloupe. Then prepare your jars for the pickle to go in. We recommend making small quantities, so two jars is adequate. Put the jars through a very hot dishwater cycle; the lids also. For good measure, dry the jars and lids for 10 minutes in a warm oven, and then place the sterilised jars on a clean tea towel, in readiness.

Take a saucepan, and add two generous slices of canteloupe melon, cut into 1 to 2 cm (½ to ¾ in) pieces. Place in the jars, leaving 1 to 2 cm (½ to ¾ in) of headspace. Once you have checked the melon fits in the jars, remove the pieces and weigh them. Then add salt, roughly a half teaspoon per jar, add some white balsamic vinegar so the tops of the melons on the jars is covered. If you wish to add black peppercorns, it is a good idea to cook them in a small pan for a minute or so in the vinegar, and then allow this to cool before adding to the melon. Do not overcook, or else the vinegar will evaporate.

Place the filled jars in the fridge and leave to generate flavour overnight. The pickles last for about a fortnight. Good with cheese for a simple lunch.

Watermelon Ice Cubes

A quick and easy way to use up a glut of watermelon. Simply remove

Melon and Thyme Pickle

the flesh from a watermelon and de-seed. Place in a blender or juicer and blend until smooth. Pour into ice cube trays and freeze. Great for adding colour and flavour to cocktails and non-alcoholic drinks.

Watermelon Mint Julep

Evoking the sultry days of the American South where the watermelon found its home is this classic cocktail with a twist coming from the fruit ice cubes.

Ingredients:
2 measures (50 ml or ⅛ pint) of bourbon
10 mint leaves plus a sprig to garnish
1 tsp of sugar syrup
4 dashes of Angostura bitters
soda water
equal amounts of watermelon ice cubes and water-based ice cubes

Add the mint leaves, sugar syrup and Angostura bitters into a highball glass and muddle together to release the flavours. Add the bourbon followed by equal quantities of watermelon ice cubes and water-based ones. Top up with soda water and finish with the sprig of mint and a straw. The watermelon ice cubes will melt before the water ones releasing their flavour into the cocktail.

Marrow Rum

Missed picking a courgette that was hidden and it has now grown too big to be worth eating? Been on holiday and the neighbour did not pick your courgettes and they have turned into marrows? With some basic home-brewing equipment you can make them into a lovely vegetable wine. The demerara sugar and raisins provide depth of flavour and the hue of golden rum. The marrow can be replaced with squash if preferred. This recipe is based on one from Judith Glover's excellent book on home winemaking, *Drink Your Own Garden*.

Ingredients:
2.3 kg (5 lb) ripe marrow (or squash)
1.4 kg (3 lb) demerara sugar
2 oranges
200 g (7 oz) of raisins
28 g (1 oz) fresh root ginger
1 Campden tablet
1 tsp of pectin enzyme
4.5 l (9.5 pints) water
wine yeast
yeast nutrient

Wash the marrows, peel and slice them (do not remove seeds) into a vessel, such as a large sterilised tub or bucket, peel and bruise the ginger, add this to the vessel along with 3.4 litres (7 pints) of cold water. Crush the Campden tablet and add this and the pectin enzyme, and stir well. Cover with a clean tea towel and leave for 24 hours.

The next day, bring 1.1 litres (2.5 pints) of water to the boil and dissolve the sugar in it. Cool to around 35 to 40°C and then add to the marrow water mixture, together with the yeast, yeast nutrient and the juice of the two oranges.

Re-cover and keep in a warm place to ferment for five days, stirring a couple of times a day. The rum should be actively fermenting at this stage with bubbles on the surface. After five days, strain the liquid carefully off the pulp and transfer to a demi-john (or fermenting jar) and fit an airlock.

When the liquid starts to clear, transfer it to another demi-john leaving behind the sediment. This process, called racking, might need to be done more than once to get it clear, but do not rush into racking multiple times unless necessary.

When the fermentation has ended and the rum is clear, bottle and store in a cool dark place to mature for at least six months. If you try it before then you will only be disappointed. Vegetable wines (and rums) take patience to achieve a good depth of flavour.

MELON AND GOOSEBERRY JAM

This recipe makes a wonderful jam which can be eaten with cold chicken, used as a sweet jam on scones with cream, or just spooned from the bowl. It is best to consume it within two weeks, and keep refridgerated. The basic rule with jams is to use equal amounts of fruit to sugar, and add lemon juice to assist with the setting of the jam. It is also a good idea to use preserving sugar, which is granulated. And it is wise to make a small quantity, so half a melon is perfectly adequate.

Ingredients:
250 g (9 oz) or ½ a ripe melon
250 g (9 oz) preserving sugar
250 g (9 oz) fresh gooseberries, topped and tailed

Cook the fruit, chopped finely, in a pan with the sugar. The gooseberries are quite liquid when they cook, so you may not need to add any water, but watch and stir continuously. The jam is ready when a small quantity put on a saucer solidifies. Pour the jam into sterilised jars, or just into a nice bowl ready to be offered to your guests.

MELONS & OTHER CUCURBITS

Melon and Gooseberry Jam

Watermelon Salsa

Watermelon Salsa

Ingredients (serves 4):
1 slice of watermelon
an equal quantity of cucumber
1 spring onion (scallion) or a sweet red onion, or a shallot
4 very small tomatoes, finely diced
diced herbs to taste, for example basil, mint or oregano
2 limes, juiced

Take a slice of watermelon, dice it very finely, having removed all the black seeds. You can leave the very small white ones as they are hardly noticeable. Add the same amount of diced cucumber, which you can peel if you do not like the bitter skin. Add a very finely sliced spring onion (scallion), or a shallot, and the small tomatoes. Add the lime juice and the chopped herbs, and if you wish for heat, a very finely chopped red chilli with the seeds removed.

Melon Sorbet

A perfect way to bring back memories of summer harvests and to preserve the fresh flavour of a ripe melon when there is a glut of fruit. '*Noir des Carmes*' is a good choice as it is one of the most prolific producers, contains very juicy flesh and makes a striking bright orange sorbet.

Ingredients:
700 g (25 oz) whole ripe melon (or may require two melons)
8 tbsp water
6 tbsp caster sugar
3 tbsp lemon juice

Galia Melon with Manouri Cheese

In a small saucepan add the water and sugar, heat gently and stir until the sugar has dissolved, then remove from the heat. Allow to cool.

Remove the melon flesh from the skin and remove any seeds. Place into a blender along with the cooled sugar syrup and lemon juice. Blend until smooth.

Process in an ice cream maker if using, if not then pour into a freezer-safe container, such as a plastic takeaway container with a lid, and place in the freezer compartment. Every hour for the first four or five hours remove and stir vigorously to break up any ice crystals that have formed, and then return to the freezer until completely frozen.

For best serving results remove from the freezer and let it stand for up to 30 minutes at room temperature to soften, and then scoop out the portions required before returning to the freezer. Garnish with a sprig of fresh mint.

Galia Melon With Manouri Cheese, And Dates On Skewers

This is a very easy recipe and could be either a buffet starter or dessert. The taste is both sweet and salty, so it has a tendency to make you thirsty. Have plenty of iced water to hand. The cheese used here is one from Greece, a mix of sheep and goat's milk, but any hard sheep or goat's cheese would work very well.

Ingredients:
one small Galia melon
mild olive oil for frying
6 dried dates (preferably Medjool)

one Manouri cheese made of sheep's and goat's milk, or a
    different hard cheese
wooden skewers

Fry the cheese lightly in the olive oil for about two minutes. Turn it
when it is golden brown but definitely not overcooked.

Slice the melon, deseed, and cut into chunks. Cut the dates into
small pieces, around four per date.

Insert the cheese, melon and dates onto the skewers, arrange on
a plate, and serve.

Watermelon and Couscous Salad

Ingredients:
100 g (4 oz) couscous
a slice of watermelon
half a diced red onion
20 sliced black olives
a handful of sultanas
a handful of fresh mint leaves or other fresh herbs you have to hand
a glug of a good quality olive oil
the juice of two lemons
salt and pepper to taste

Cook the couscous quickly in boiling water that just covers the
grains. This should take one minute, and fluff the couscous with a
fork to make sure it does not stick to the pan. Place the couscous
in a bowl, and let it cool.

Slice the other ingredients finely, and add to the couscous, with
a good glug of olive oil and fresh herbs – a handful of fresh mint
leaves, for example – and the lemon juice. Season and serve.

Squash with Couscous, Walnuts and Cinnamon

As we move into the autumn, the squashes and pumpkins start to appear in the farmer's markets, and hopefully a few in your garden or allotment. Here is a recipe you may not have thought about for using these lovely vegetables.

Ingredients (serves 2)
1 small squash, the striped variety acorn squash 'Sweet Dumpling'
  (Cucurbita pepo) is a fine one
100 g (4 oz) couscous
4 dried dates, finely chopped
10 or so walnuts, finely chopped
1 tsp cinnamon, or more to taste
3 tbsp stock, chicken or vegetable
3 tbsp pomegranate molasses
light olive oil and hot water to add moisture while cooking
salt to taste

Divide the small squash in half, remove the seeds and stringy flesh, and place in a shallow baking tray. Add salt, light olive oil (about 3 tablespoons), and a cup of boiled water to the pan, so you braise the squash. Cook for 40 minutes in a moderate oven (160°C or gas mark 4) until the squash is tender. Test this with a knife from time to time. In the meantime, cook the couscous in a pan on the hob. Add hot water to the pan, just covering the grains, and heat for half a minute. Turn off the heat and let the water be absorbed, and it will cook on its own. Fluff up with a fork, and add the cinnamon, chopped dates and walnuts, and any other ingredients you have to hand (pine nuts and pomegranate seeds would be good alternatives).

Fill the cooked squash halves and bake in the oven for 10 to 15 minutes and serve. Make sure you have enough water added to make a sauce, and drizzle pomegranate molasses over the squash just before you serve. Scatter leaves of spinach or chard if you have them to hand.

ACKNOWLEDGEMENTS

I would like to thank my family for their unwavering belief in me, support and endless patience when I get involved in these projects. Catheryn Kilgarriff and Brendan King at Prospect Books for believing in the idea and making a first-time author feel so comfortable. Also to Catheryn Kilgarriff for her contributions of recipes and photographs on pages 174 to 186. The staff and students at Wakefield College for helping me to grow the range of cucurbits necessary for this book. Rob Mcelwee for setting up and administering the Heirloom Cucurbits Facebook group, and for his advice and that of the other group members. Victor Garcia Moreno at Semillas la Peba who replied to my appeal on the group and provided me with seeds of '*Hero of Lockinge*', his guidance, support and patience, particularly throughout my first failed year of trying to cultivate this precious melon, was invaluable. Linda MacKechnie for her incredible work cataloguing cucurbit varieties and her willingness to share it for free on her website (www.ilplntgrl.com). The University of Reading and the Museum of English Rural Life for maintaining the Suttons archive and allowing me to view the old seed catalogues. Hilary Wood at Blenheim Palace for providing me with historical information about '*Blenheim Orange*'. The Northern Fruit Group for their tireless work encouraging and supporting people to grow fruit, and their efforts to identify and safeguard old varieties. Garden Organic and the Heritage Seed Library for their dedication and skill in preserving and sharing heritage varieties of vegetables and fruit which would otherwise have been lost.

BIBLIOGRAPHY

Baker, Harry. *RHS Growing Fruit*, Octopus, 2011.

Beazley, Mitchell. *RHS Growing Vegetables & Herbs*, Index Books, 2014.

Brookshaw, George. *The Book of Fruits*, Taschen, 2005.

Davies, Jennifer. *The Victorian Kitchen Garden*, BBC Books, 1987.

Flowerdew, Bob. *Grown Your Own, Eat Your Own*, Kyle Cathie, 2008.

Gettle, Jere & Emilee. *The Heirloom Life Gardener,* Hyperion, 2011.

Goldmand, Amy. *The Melon*, City Point Press, 2019.

Hessayon, D. G. Dr. *The Fruit Herb Expert*, Transworld, 1993.

Hessayon, D. G. Dr. *The Vegetable and Herb Expert*, Expert Books, 2003.

Phillips, Roger & Rix, Martyn. *Vegetables*, Macmillan Reference Books, 1995.

ONLINE RESOURCES

Baker Creek Heirloom Seeds (www.rareseeds.com)

Garden Organic & Heritage Seed Library (gardenorganic.org.uk/hsl)

Heirloom Cucurbits Facebook Group (www.facebook.com/groups/950816328591402/)

Irish Seed Savers Association (irishseedsavers.ie)

Museum of English Rural Life (merl.reading.ac.uk)

Northern Fruit Group (www.thenorthernfruitgroup.com)

RHS Fruit Group (www.thefruitgroup.org.uk)

Real Seeds (www.realseeds.co.uk)

Richard Brown's Blog (thehorticulturaltherapist.wordpress.com)

Richard Brown on Twitter (@richardbrownht)

Seed Savers Exchange (www.seedsavers.org)

Seeds of Diversity Canada (seeds.ca)

Thomas Etty Seeds (www.thomasetty.co.uk)

Wakefield College Horticulture (www.wakefield.ac.uk/study-with-us/subject-areas/horticulture)

INDEX OF RECIPES

INDEX